# 1949 U.S.

## YEARBOOK

ISBN: 9781790461134

This book gives a fascinating and informative insight into life in the United States in 1949. It includes everything from the most popular music of the year to the cost of a buying a new house. Additionally there are chapters covering people in high office, the best-selling films of the year and all the main news and events. Want to know who won the World Series or which U.S. personalities were born in 1949? All this and much more awaits you within.

© Liberty Eagle Publishing Ltd. 2018
All Rights Reserved

# INDEX

**FIRST EDITION**

# 1949

## January

| S | M | T | W | T | F | S |
|---|---|---|---|---|---|---|
|   |   |   |   |   |   | 1 |
| 2 | 3 | 4 | 5 | 6 | 7 | 8 |
| 9 | 10 | 11 | 12 | 13 | 14 | 15 |
| 16 | 17 | 18 | 19 | 20 | 21 | 22 |
| 23 | 24 | 25 | 26 | 27 | 28 | 29 |
| 30 | 31 |   |   |   |   |   |

◑:7  ○:14  ◐:21  ●:28

## February

| S | M | T | W | T | F | S |
|---|---|---|---|---|---|---|
|   |   | 1 | 2 | 3 | 4 | 5 |
| 6 | 7 | 8 | 9 | 10 | 11 | 12 |
| 13 | 14 | 15 | 16 | 17 | 18 | 19 |
| 20 | 21 | 22 | 23 | 24 | 25 | 26 |
| 27 | 28 |   |   |   |   |   |

◑:6  ○:13  ◐:19  ●:27

## March

| S | M | T | W | T | F | S |
|---|---|---|---|---|---|---|
|   |   | 1 | 2 | 3 | 4 | 5 |
| 6 | 7 | 8 | 9 | 10 | 11 | 12 |
| 13 | 14 | 15 | 16 | 17 | 18 | 19 |
| 20 | 21 | 22 | 23 | 24 | 25 | 26 |
| 27 | 28 | 29 | 30 | 31 |   |   |

◑:7  ○:14  ◐:21  ●:29

## April

| S | M | T | W | T | F | S |
|---|---|---|---|---|---|---|
|   |   |   |   |   | 1 | 2 |
| 3 | 4 | 5 | 6 | 7 | 8 | 9 |
| 10 | 11 | 12 | 13 | 14 | 15 | 16 |
| 17 | 18 | 19 | 20 | 21 | 22 | 23 |
| 24 | 25 | 26 | 27 | 28 | 29 | 30 |

◑:6  ○:12  ◐:19  ●:28

## May

| S | M | T | W | T | F | S |
|---|---|---|---|---|---|---|
| 1 | 2 | 3 | 4 | 5 | 6 | 7 |
| 8 | 9 | 10 | 11 | 12 | 13 | 14 |
| 15 | 16 | 17 | 18 | 19 | 20 | 21 |
| 22 | 23 | 24 | 25 | 26 | 27 | 28 |
| 29 | 30 | 31 |   |   |   |   |

◑:5  ○:12  ◐:19  ●:27

## June

| S | M | T | W | T | F | S |
|---|---|---|---|---|---|---|
|   |   |   | 1 | 2 | 3 | 4 |
| 5 | 6 | 7 | 8 | 9 | 10 | 11 |
| 12 | 13 | 14 | 15 | 16 | 17 | 18 |
| 19 | 20 | 21 | 22 | 23 | 24 | 25 |
| 26 | 27 | 28 | 29 | 30 |   |   |

◑:3  ○:10  ◐:18  ●:26

## July

| S | M | T | W | T | F | S |
|---|---|---|---|---|---|---|
|   |   |   |   |   | 1 | 2 |
| 3 | 4 | 5 | 6 | 7 | 8 | 9 |
| 10 | 11 | 12 | 13 | 14 | 15 | 16 |
| 17 | 18 | 19 | 20 | 21 | 22 | 23 |
| 24 | 25 | 26 | 27 | 28 | 29 | 30 |
| 31 |   |   |   |   |   |   |

◑:3  ○:10  ◐:18  ●:25

## August

| S | M | T | W | T | F | S |
|---|---|---|---|---|---|---|
|   | 1 | 2 | 3 | 4 | 5 | 6 |
| 7 | 8 | 9 | 10 | 11 | 12 | 13 |
| 14 | 15 | 16 | 17 | 18 | 19 | 20 |
| 21 | 22 | 23 | 24 | 25 | 26 | 27 |
| 28 | 29 | 30 | 31 |   |   |   |

◑:1  ○:8  ◐:16  ●:23  ◑:30

## September

| S | M | T | W | T | F | S |
|---|---|---|---|---|---|---|
|   |   |   |   | 1 | 2 | 3 |
| 4 | 5 | 6 | 7 | 8 | 9 | 10 |
| 11 | 12 | 13 | 14 | 15 | 16 | 17 |
| 18 | 19 | 20 | 21 | 22 | 23 | 24 |
| 25 | 26 | 27 | 28 | 29 | 30 |   |

○:7  ◐:15  ●:22  ◑:28

## October

| S | M | T | W | T | F | S |
|---|---|---|---|---|---|---|
|   |   |   |   |   |   | 1 |
| 2 | 3 | 4 | 5 | 6 | 7 | 8 |
| 9 | 10 | 11 | 12 | 13 | 14 | 15 |
| 16 | 17 | 18 | 19 | 20 | 21 | 22 |
| 23 | 24 | 25 | 26 | 27 | 28 | 29 |
| 30 | 31 |   |   |   |   |   |

○:6  ◐:14  ●:21  ◑:28

## November

| S | M | T | W | T | F | S |
|---|---|---|---|---|---|---|
|   |   | 1 | 2 | 3 | 4 | 5 |
| 6 | 7 | 8 | 9 | 10 | 11 | 12 |
| 13 | 14 | 15 | 16 | 17 | 18 | 19 |
| 20 | 21 | 22 | 23 | 24 | 25 | 26 |
| 27 | 28 | 29 | 30 |   |   |   |

○:5  ◐:13  ●:20  ◑:27

## December

| S | M | T | W | T | F | S |
|---|---|---|---|---|---|---|
|   |   |   |   | 1 | 2 | 3 |
| 4 | 5 | 6 | 7 | 8 | 9 | 10 |
| 11 | 12 | 13 | 14 | 15 | 16 | 17 |
| 18 | 19 | 20 | 21 | 22 | 23 | 24 |
| 25 | 26 | 27 | 28 | 29 | 30 | 31 |

○:5  ◐:12  ●:19  ◑:27

# PEOPLE IN HIGH OFFICE

### Harry S. Truman
April 12, 1945 - January 20, 1953
Democratic Party

Born May 8, 1884, Truman served as the 33$^{rd}$ President of the United States succeeding to the presidency on April 12, 1945, when Roosevelt died after months of declining health. Harry S. Truman died December 26, 1972.

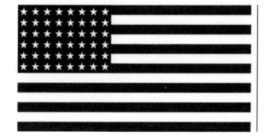

### 80$^{th}$ & 81$^{st}$ United States Congress

| | |
|---:|:---|
| Vice President | Alben W. Barkley |
| Chief Justice | Fred M. Vinson |
| Speaker of the House | Sam Rayburn |
| Senate Majority Leader | Scott W. Lucas |

U.S. Flag - 48 stars (1912-1959)

United Kingdom

Monarch
**King George VI**
Dec 11, 1936 - Feb 6, 1952

Prime Minister
**Clement Attlee**
Jul 26, 1945 - Oct 26, 1951

Australia

Canada

Ireland

Prime Minister
**Ben Chifley**
Labor Party
July 13, '45 - Dec 19, '49

Prime Minister
**Louis St. Laurent**
Liberal Party
Nov 15, '48 - Jun 21, '57

Taoiseach of Ireland
**John A. Costello**
Fine Gael
Feb 18, '48 - Jun 13, '51

6

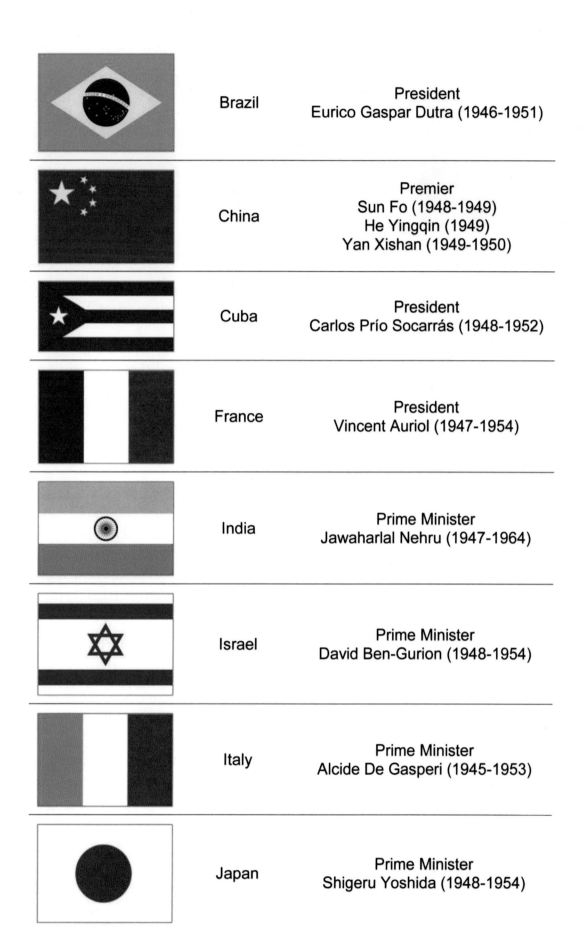

| | | |
|---|---|---|
| | Brazil | **President**<br>Eurico Gaspar Dutra (1946-1951) |
| | China | **Premier**<br>Sun Fo (1948-1949)<br>He Yingqin (1949)<br>Yan Xishan (1949-1950) |
| | Cuba | **President**<br>Carlos Prío Socarrás (1948-1952) |
| | France | **President**<br>Vincent Auriol (1947-1954) |
| | India | **Prime Minister**<br>Jawaharlal Nehru (1947-1964) |
| | Israel | **Prime Minister**<br>David Ben-Gurion (1948-1954) |
| | Italy | **Prime Minister**<br>Alcide De Gasperi (1945-1953) |
| | Japan | **Prime Minister**<br>Shigeru Yoshida (1948-1954) |

Mexico

**President**
**Miguel Alemán Valdés (1946-1952)**

New Zealand

**Prime Minister**
**Peter Fraser (1940-1949)**
**Sidney Holland (1949-1957)**

Pakistan

**Prime Minister**
**Liaquat Ali Khan (1947-1951)**

Spain

**President**
**Francisco Franco (1938-1973)**

South Africa

**Prime Minister**
**Daniel François Malan (1948-1954)**

Soviet Union

**Communist Party Leader**
**Joseph Stalin (1922-1953)**

Turkey

**Prime Minister**
**Hasan Saka (1947-1949)**
**Şemsettin Günaltay (1949-1950)**

West Germany

**Chancellor**
**Konrad Adenauer (1949-1963)**

# U.S. NEWS & EVENTS

## JAN

| | |
|---|---|
| 2 | Luis Muñoz Marín becomes the first democratically elected Governor of the U.S. unincorporated territory of Puerto Rico. |
| 2 | One of the worst blizzards on record strikes the northern Plains. It lasts for three days with the National Weather Service reporting 12 people dead in Wyoming and 28 further deaths in western South Dakota, Colorado and Nebraska. Subsequent storms through mid-February produce enormous snow drifts that paralyze much of the region. Roads and railroads are blocked so airplanes are used to bring food and medical supplies to isolated towns, and hay to livestock. On March 1, after the federal government had completed rescue operations, the official death toll for the whole region stood at 76. |

January 4 - RMS Caronia of the Cunard Line departs Southampton, England for New York on her maiden voyage. Launched on the October 30, 1947 by HRH The Princess Elizabeth and completed in December 1948, she served with Cunard until 1967. She was nicknamed the Green Goddess and is credited as one of the first dual-purpose built ships: suited to cruising, but also capable of transatlantic crossings.

| | |
|---|---|
| 5 | President Harry S. Truman unveils his Fair Deal program in his State of the Union Address to Congress. The Fair Deal was an ambitious set of proposals to continue New Deal liberalism but with the Conservative Coalition controlling Congress only a few of its major initiatives actually became law. According to Richard Neustadt some of the most important proposals outlined were; aid to education, universal health insurance, the Fair Employment Practices Commission, and repeal of the Taft–Hartley Act - these were all debated at length and then voted down. |
| 6 | The first photos of genes are taken with an electron microscope, by assistant professor of anatomy Daniel C. Pease and assistant professor of experimental medicine Richard F. Baker, at the University of Southern California. |

**JAN**

| | |
|---|---|
| 10 | RCA Victor introduces the first 45rpm, 7 inch record. |
| 10-11 | Los Angeles, California receives its first measurable recorded snowfall (⅓ inch). |
| 17 | The first Volkswagen Beetle arrives in the United States and is brought to New York City by Dutch businessman Ben Pon. Pon peddled the car up and down the East Coast hoping to strike a deal with any interested dealers. Three weeks later he gave up and sold the Beetle for exactly $800 to settle his bill at the Roosevelt Hotel. 1949 ended with just two Beetles sold. In 1950 Austrian born Max Hoffman became the official importer and sold 157 Beetles. From this auspicious start the Beetle would go on to become an American automotive phenomenon. |
| 25 | The first Emmy Awards are presented at the Hollywood Athletic Club in Los Angeles, California. The winners include Shirley Dinsdale, Pantomime Quiz (KTLA) and the made for television film, The Necklace. |

**FEB**

Left: DiMaggio with his brothers Vince and Dom before the start of the 1936 World Series.
Right: DiMaggio and future wife Marilyn Monroe at Chasen's, West Hollywood (1953).

February 7 - New York Yankees Joe DiMaggio signs a contract to become the first baseball player to break $100,000 in earnings a year. During his career he was a three-time AL MVP Award winner and an All-Star in each of his 13 seasons. DiMaggio also won ten American League pennants and nine World Series championships, but is perhaps best known for his 56-game hitting streak (May 15 - July 16, 1941), a record that still stands today.

| | |
|---|---|
| 10 | Arthur Miller's tragedy, Death of a Salesman, opens at the Morosco Theatre on Broadway in New York City, with Lee J. Cobb in the title role of Willy Loman. The play runs for 742 performances and receives the 1949 Pulitzer Prize for Drama and Tony Award for Best Play. Today is widely considered to be one of the greatest plays of the 20th century. |
| 19 | Ezra Pound is controversially awarded the first Bollingen Prize, a new national poetry award by the Library of Congress. He received $1,000 in prize money which had been donated by the wealthy and influential Mellon family from Pittsburgh, Pennsylvania. |
| 22 | Grady, a 1,200-pound cow, gets stuck inside a silo on a farm in Yukon, Oklahoma. When owner Bill Mach asks for help through his local newspaper Grady becomes national news featuring in both Life and TIME magazines. Grady was eventually freed after being covered in 10lbs of axel grease and squeezed through the silo opening. |
| 24 | A V-2/WAC-Corporal rocket becomes the first object to reach 5x the speed of sound at White Sands Missile Range near Las Cruces, New Mexico. |

| | |
|---|---|
| 2 | The B-50 Superfortress Lucky Lady II lands in Fort Worth, Texas, after completing the first non-stop around-the-world airplane flight. It was refuelled in flight four times during the journey and was flown by Captain James Gallagher. |
| 2 | The world's first automatic street lights become operational in New Milford, Connecticut. |
| 17 | The Shamrock Hotel in Houston, Texas, owned by oil tycoon Glenn McCarthy, has its grand opening. It was the largest hotel built in the United States during the 1940s and the grand opening is still cited as one of the biggest social events ever held in Houston. |

March 20 - The California Zephyr passenger train goes into service between Chicago and Oakland, California, and is the first long distance train to feature Vista Dome cars as regular equipment. For the inaugural run every woman on the train was given silver and orange orchids flown in from Hilo, Hawaii. The car hostesses, known as Zephyrettes, had to fulfil a variety of criteria including being single, and being a college graduate or registered nurse. They were also expected to conduct themselves with dignity and poise, and refrain from smoking or drinking in uniform.

# MAR

26     The first half of Giuseppe Verdi's opera Aida, conducted by legendary conductor Arturo Toscanini, is telecast by NBC live from Studio 8H at Rockefeller Center. The second half is telecast a week later. This is the only complete opera that Toscanini ever conducts on television.

28     James Forrestal, the first U.S. Secretary of Defense, resigns suddenly. He is replaced by Louis A. Johnson who is an ardent supporter of President Truman's defense retrenchment policy.

29     The 21st Academy Awards are held at the Academy Theater in Hollywood, California. The ceremony awarded Oscars for the best in films in 1948 and featured a number of firsts. Amongst other things, it was the first time a non-Hollywood production (Hamlet) had won Best Picture and the first time an individual (Laurence Olivier) had directed themself in an Oscar-winning performance.

# APR

4     The United States and 11 other nations establish the North Atlantic Treaty Organization (NATO), a mutual defence pact aimed at containing possible Soviet aggression against Western Europe.

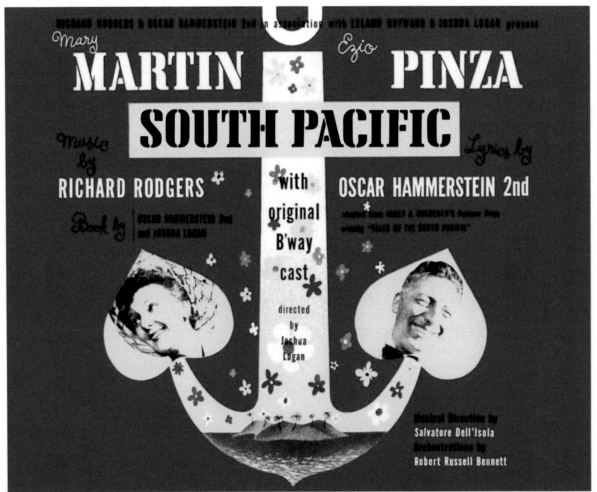

April 7 - Rodgers and Hammerstein's South Pacific, starring Mary Martin and Ezio Pinza, opens on Broadway. It goes on to become their second longest-running musical and an instant classic of the musical theatre. The score's biggest hit song is Some Enchanted Evening.

# APR

**13**    A 6.7Mw earthquake occurs in the area between Olympia and Tacoma, Washington, and is felt throughout the state as well as parts of Oregon, British Columbia, Idaho, and Montana. It is the largest recorded earthquake to occur in the Puget Sound region of Washington and resulted in the deaths of eight people. The total damage from the earthquake was estimated at $25 million.

**23**    The USS United States (CVA-58), which was to be the lead ship of a new design of aircraft carrier, is cancelled. It is one of five supercarriers (that were approved for construction on July 29, 1948) that were cancelled, causing high-ranking Navy officials to resign in protest in what has been called the Revolt of the Admirals.

# MAY

**3**    The first Viking rocket, built by the Glenn L. Martin Company (now Lockheed-Martin) under the direction of the U.S. Naval Research Laboratory (NRL), is launched. It reaches an altitude of 50 miles but is limited by a premature engine cut-off which is eventually traced to steam leakage from the turbine casing. In all, twelve Viking rockets flew between 1949 and 1955, with an aim of providing an independent U.S. capability in rocketry and to provide a vehicle better suited to scientific research.

# JUN

**8**    A report by the Federal Bureau of Investigation names well-known Hollywood figures as members of the Communist Party, setting off a period of paranoia known as the Red Scare Two. Among those on the report's list were Frederic March, John Garfield, Paul Muni, Edward G. Robinson, Paul Robeson, and the writer Dorothy Parker.

**11**    Albert, a rhesus monkey, becomes the first primate astronaut after riding to a height of over 39 miles on a V-2 rocket. Albert unfortunately dies of suffocation during the flight.

**14**    Albert II, on board another V-2 rocket, becomes the first primate in space. He reaches an altitude of 83 miles (134km) but dies on impact after a parachute failure. Astronauts Albert III and Albert IV were also launched on V-2 rockets later in 1949 but tragically Albert III died at 35,000ft in an explosion and Albert IV in another parachute failure.

June 19 - The inaugural NASCAR Strictly Stock Series Race takes place at the Charlotte Speedway in Charlotte, North Carolina. The race comprised 200 laps on a 0.75-mile dirt oval with Bob Flock taking the pole position with a top speed of 67.958mph. Glenn Dunaway initially claimed the victory in his 1947 Ford but was later disqualified because his car had spread rear springs. The win was instead awarded to Jim Roper driving a 1949 Lincoln.

## JUN

| | |
|---|---|
| 22 | Ezzard Charles beats Jersey Joe Walcott in 15 rounds to take the National Boxing Association (NBA) world heavyweight title. Walcott would retake the title from Charles on July 18, 1951. |
| 24 | The first television western, Hopalong Cassidy starring William Boyd, airs on NBC. |

## JUL

| | |
|---|---|
| 5 | The New York Giants purchase Monty Irvin and Henry Thompson, their first African American players. |
| 10 | The first practical rectangular TV tube is announced in Toledo, Ohio. |

## AUG

| | |
|---|---|
| 3 | The Basketball Association of America and National Basketball League merge to form National Basketball Association. |
| 5 | The U.S. Department of State publishes The China White Paper arguing that American intervention in China is doomed to failure. The paper helps to convince many critics that the administration has failed to check the spread of communism in China. |
| 10 | The National Military Establishment (formerly the Department of War) is renamed the Department of Defense. |
| 16 | The Office of Chairman of the Joint Chiefs of Staff is created. General of the Army, Omar Bradley, becomes the highest-ranking and senior-most military officer in the U.S. Armed Forces, and the principal military advisor to the President. |

August 28 - Six of the last sixteen surviving veterans of the American Civil War meet in Indianapolis at the 82nd and final Grand Army of the Republic (GAR) encampment. They are Albert Woolson (102), Robert Barrett (102), Theodore A. Penland (100), James A. Hard (108), Joseph Clovese (105) and Charles L. Chappel (102).

| | |
|---|---|
| 6 | Howard Unruh, a World War II veteran, kills 13 neighbors (including three children) during a 12-minute walk through his neighborhood in Camden, New Jersey. Using a souvenir Luger he becomes America's first single-episode mass murderer. Unruh was found to be criminally insane and died in 2009, at the age of 88, following 60 years of confinement. |
| 15 | The Housing Act of 1949, a landmark sweeping expansion of the federal role in mortgage insurance and issuance, and the construction of public housing, is enacted. |

September 15 - The hugely popular Lone Ranger series premieres on ABC. Starring Clayton Moore in the titular role and Jay Silverheels as Tonto, the show would run for a total of 5 seasons and 221 episodes.

| | |
|---|---|
| 28 | The movie My Friend Irma is released and premiere's in New York City. It is most notable as the film debut of the comedy duo of Dean Martin and Jerry Lewis, and is the first of 12 movies they will make together. |
| 29 | American Iva Toguri D'Aquino is found guilty of treason for broadcasting English-language propaganda for Japan as 'Tokyo Rose' during World War II. She spent more than six years out of a ten-year sentence in prison. Journalistic and governmental investigators years later pieced together the history of irregularities with the indictment, trial and conviction, and Toguri received a pardon in 1977 from President Gerald Ford. |
| 30 | The Berlin Airlift comes to an end after 15 months. The Airlift started as a result of the Berlin Blockade which was one of the first major international crises of the Cold War. Aircrews from the United States, Britain, Canada, Australia, New Zealand and South Africa flew over 200,000 flights in one year providing the West Berliners with up to 8,893 tons of necessities each day. By the end of the operation 17 American and 7 British planes had crashed delivering supplies to Soviet blockaded Berlin, and a total of 101 fatalities had been recorded (these were mostly due to non-flying accidents and included 31 Americans and 40 Britons). |

# OCT

| | |
|---|---|
| 3 | WERD, the first radio station owned and programmed by African Americans, is established in Atlanta, Georgia. Owner Jesse B. Blayton Sr. purchased WERD for $50,000 and hired his son Jesse Jr. as station manager. 'Jockey' Jack Gibson was hired and by 1951 he was the most popular DJ in Atlanta. |

## OCT

**14** | 14 U.S. Communist Party leaders are convicted of sedition. At the time it was the longest federal trial in U.S. history and was heavily reported on by magazines, newspapers and the radio.

**27** | An airliner flying from Paris to New York City crashes into a mountain while attempting to land at Santa Maria Airport in the Azores island of São Miguel. All 48 people on board are killed including violinist Ginette Neveu and boxer Marcel Cerdan.

## NOV

**4** | One Man's Family premieres on television. The series was based on the long running (1932-1959) radio soap opera of the same name (the longest-running uninterrupted dramatic serial in the history of American radio).

**8-12** | Race riots start in Englewood, Chicago, Illinois, caused by rumors and misinformation that blacks, Jews and communists were planning to take over their neighborhood. At its peak there were 10,000 rioters with police doing little to stop the violence. Over the five days of troubles at least thirteen people were beaten severely enough to be hospitalised.

November 18 - Jackie Robinson, the first African American to play in Major League Baseball (MLB) in the modern era, wins National League MVP.

**21** | Bill Veeck sells the Cleveland Indians for $22 million to a syndicate headed by insurance magnate Ellis Ryan.

**24** | The Squaw Valley Ski Resort, California officially opens. Today it is one of the largest ski areas in the U.S. and since joining with Alpine Meadows in 2012, the resorts offer joint access to 6,200 acres, 43 lifts and over 270 trails.

**25** | Ted Williams, regarded as one of the greatest players in baseball history, wins the American League MVP for the second time (also 1946).

## DEC

**8** | MGM release On the Town, the film adaptation of the Broadway musical, starring Gene Kelly, Frank Sinatra, Ann Miller and Vera-Ellen. The film was an immediate success and won the Academy Award for Best Scoring of a Musical Picture.

**21** | The movie Samson and Delilah, directed and produced by Cecil B. DeMille, starring Hedy Lamarr and Victor Mature, premieres in New York. Praised upon its release it receives five Academy Award nominations and wins both Best Art Direction and Best Costume Design.

**29** | KC2XAK of Bridgeport, Connecticut, becomes the first UHF television station to operate a regular daily schedule.

# 1949 NOTABLE U.S. DEATHS

| | |
|---|---|
| Jan 6 | Victor Lonzo Fleming (b. February 23, 1889) - Academy Award winning film director, cinematographer and producer, whose most popular films were The Wizard of Oz (1939) and Gone with the Wind (1939). |
| Feb 1 | Herbert P. Stothart (b. September 11, 1885) - Songwriter, arranger and conductor who was widely acknowledged as one of the top composers of his time. |
| Feb 17 | Ellery Harding Clark (b. March 13, 1874) - Track and field athlete who was the first modern Olympic champion in high jump and long jump. |
| Mar 7 | Sol Bloom (b. March 9, 1870) - Politician from New York who served fourteen terms in the United States House of Representatives (1923 until his death in 1949). |
| Mar 7 | Bradbury Norton Robinson, Jr. (b. February 1, 1884) - Pioneering American football player who threw the first forward pass in American football history (1906). |
| Mar 25 | Jack Kapp (b. June 15, 1901) - Record company executive with Brunswick Records who founded the American Decca Records in 1934 and oversaw Bing Crosby's rise to success as a recording artist. |
| Apr 15 | Wallace Fitzgerald Beery (b. April 1, 1885) - Academy Award winning film actor who appeared in some 250 movies during a 36-year career. |
| Apr 22 | Charles B. Middleton (b. October 3, 1874) - Stage and film actor who started in film at the age of 46. During a career that lasted almost 30 years he went on to make over 200 films. Middleton is perhaps best remembered for his role as the villainous emperor Ming the Merciless in the three Flash Gordon serials made between 1936 and 1940. |
| May 22 | James Vincent Forrestal (b. February 15, 1892) - The last Cabinet-level U.S. Secretary of the Navy and the first U.S. Secretary of Defense. |

American cartoonist, entrepreneur **Robert LeRoy Ripley** passed away on May 27, 1949

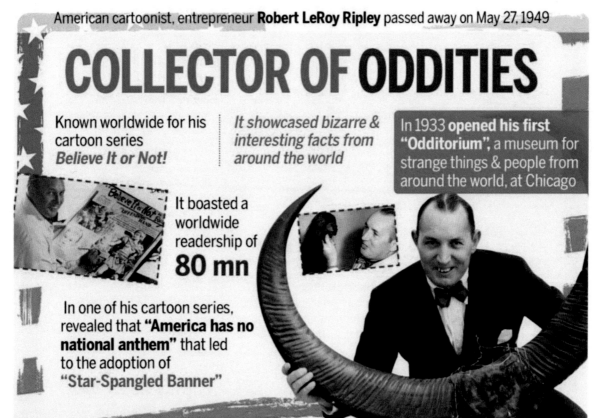

# COLLECTOR OF ODDITIES

Known worldwide for his cartoon series *Believe It or Not!*

*It showcased bizarre & interesting facts from around the world*

In 1933 **opened his first "Odditorium"**, a museum for strange things & people from around the world, at Chicago

It boasted a worldwide readership of **80 mn**

In one of his cartoon series, revealed that **"America has no national anthem"** that led to the adoption of **"Star-Spangled Banner"**

May 27 - Robert LeRoy Ripley (b. December 25, 1890) - Cartoonist, entrepreneur and amateur anthropologist who is known for creating the Ripley's Believe It or Not! newspaper panel series, and radio and television shows, which featured odd facts from around the world.

| | |
|---|---|
| Jun 25 | John Frank 'Buck' Freeman (b. October 30, 1871) - Major League Baseball right fielder at the turn of the 20th century who was one of the top sluggers of his era. His most famous feat was the 25 home runs he hit during the 1899 season. |
| Aug 16 | Margaret Munnerlyn Mitchell (b. November 8, 1900) - Author and journalist. Only one novel by Mitchell was published during her lifetime, the American Civil War-era classic, Gone with the Wind, for which she won the National Book Award for Most Distinguished Novel of 1936 and the Pulitzer Prize for Fiction in 1937. |
| Sep 12 | Henry Thacker 'Harry' Burleigh (b. December 2, 1866) - Classical composer, arranger and professional singer known for his baritone voice. In 1917 he received the Spingarn Medal, awarded for outstanding achievement by an African American. |
| Sep 18 | Frank Morgan (b. Francis Phillip Wuppermann; June 1, 1890) - Character actor who is best known as a Metro-Goldwyn-Mayer contract player and as the titular character in The Wizard of Oz (1939). |
| Sep 22 | Samuel Grosvenor Wood (b. July 10, 1883) - Film director and producer, best known for directing such Hollywood hits as A Night at the Opera (1935), A Day at the Races (1937), Goodbye, Mr. Chips (1939), and The Pride of the Yankees (1942). |
| Oct 1 | Buddy Clark (b. July 26, 1912) - Popular singer of the 1930s and 1940s. After Clark's return from service in World War II his career blossomed and he became one of the nation's top crooners. |
| Oct 23 | Almanzo James Wilder (b. February 13, 1857) - Husband of Laura Ingalls Wilder and the father of Rose Wilder Lane, both noted American writers. |
| Oct 31 | Edward Reilly Stettinius Jr. (b. October 22, 1900) - Businessman who served as U.S. Secretary of State under Presidents Franklin D. Roosevelt and Harry S. Truman (1944-1945), and as U.S. Ambassador to the United Nations (1945-1946). |

November 25 - Bill 'Bojangles' Robinson (b. May 25, 1878) - Tap dancer and actor who was the best known and most highly paid African-American entertainer in the first half of the 20th century. His long career mirrored changes in American entertainment tastes and technology. He started in the age of minstrel shows and moved into vaudeville, Broadway, the recording industry, Hollywood, radio and television.

| | |
|---|---|
| Dec 6 | Huddie William Ledbetter (b. January 20, 1888) - Rock and Roll Hall of Fame (1988) folk and blues musician best known as Lead Belly. He is notable for his strong vocals, virtuosity on the twelve-string guitar, and the folk standards he introduced. |
| Dec 25 | Leon Schlesinger (b. May 20, 1884) - Film producer who founded Leon Schlesinger Studios, which later became the Warner Bros. Cartoons studio, during the golden age of American animation. |

1 | January 25 - David Ben-Gurion's Mapai party win the first Israeli legislative election with 35.7% of the vote.
2 | March 8 - Australian Donald George Bradman plays his last innings in first class cricket, scoring 30. Often referred to as 'The Don', he is widely acknowledged as the greatest batsman of all time. Bradman's career Test batting average of 99.94 is often cited as the greatest achievement by any sportsman in any major sport.
3 | April 18 - Ireland formally becomes a republic and leaves the British Commonwealth.

April 24 - The Manchester Mark 1 computer becomes operational at the Victoria University of Manchester, England. It is one of the earliest stored-program computers and its successful operation is widely reported in the British press who use the phrase, electronic brain, in describing it to their readers.

5 | May 4 - An Italian Airlines Fiat G.212, carrying the entire Torino F.C. football team, crashes into the back wall of the Basilica of Superga killing all 31 people on board.
6 | May 9 - Prince Rainier III becomes monarch of Monaco. His coronation as 30th ruling Prince of Monaco takes place later in the year on November 19.
7 | May 11 - Siam renames itself Thailand.
8 | May 11 - Israel becomes 59th member of UN by a vote of 37-12.
9 | June 8 - George Orwell's dystopian novel Nineteen Eighty-Four is published in London by Secker & Warburg. Considered to be one of the most influential novels written during the twentieth century, the story focused on a futuristic totalitarian state that set out to control the thoughts of its citizens and rewrite history. The novel was an immediate success and was made into a movie in 1956 and 1984. The book was so influential that many of its made up terms have become part of normal speech, such as Big Brother, Thought Police and doublethink.
10 | July 8 - South Africa's National Party begins implementing apartheid with the Prohibition of Mixed Marriages Act, prohibiting a white person to marrying a person of another race. Subsequent legislation, especially the Population Registration and Immorality Acts of 1950, facilitated its implementation by requiring all individuals living in South Africa to register as a member of one of four officially defined racial groups and prohibiting extramarital sexual relationships between whites and people of different races.
11 | July 27 - The British-built DeHavilland Comet, the world's first commercial passenger jet airliner, makes its maiden flight at Hatfield in Hertfordshire, England. After that first flight (which lasted for about thirty minutes) they continued to test the Comet and build prototypes until its commercial introduction in 1952. It was predicted to be a financial success but soon after its debut the Comet began suffering from several mechanical malfunctions, including incidents in which the jet broke up in mid-flight. After extensive research the problems were traced and the Comet redesigned. It remained in production in some form until the 1990's.

# CONTINUED

| | |
|---|---|
| 12 | August 5 - The Ambato earthquake in Ecuador, measuring 6.8 on the Richter scale, kills more than 5,000 people. The quake causes heavy damage to the city of Ambato and also destroys the nearby villages of Guano, Patate, Pelileo and Pillaro. |
| 13 | August 29 - The USSR secretly performs its first nuclear test at the Semipalatinsk in Kazakhstan. Code named 'First Lightning' by the Soviets and 'Joe 1' by the Americans, the weapons' design was very similar to the plutonium bomb that was dropped on Nagasaki, Japan, in 1945. |
| 14 | September 2 - The movie The Third Man, directed by Carol Reed, starring Joseph Cotten, Alida Valli and Orson Welles, is released in the United Kingdom. It would go on to win the Academy Award for Best Cinematography in 1950, and in 1999 the British Film Institute would vote The Third Man the greatest British film of all time. |
| 15 | September 15 - Konrad Adenauer is elected as the first Chancellor of the new created Federal Republic of Germany. |
| 16 | The British government devalues the pound by 30% against the U.S dollar (from $4.03 to $2.80). This major economic development subsequently causes 9 other countries to follow suit. |
| 17 | October 7 - The German Democratic Republic is formed from the Soviet occupation zone in Germany. Four days later Wilhelm Pieck is elected its first President. |
| 18 | November 29 - Ophthalmologist Sir Nicholas Harold Lloyd Ridley, a pioneer of intraocular lens surgery for cataract patients, achieves the first, albeit temporary, implant of an intraocular lens at St Thomas' Hospital, London. Just a couple of months later, on February 8, 1950, he would go on to implant a permanent artificial lens into an eye. |
| 19 | December 8 - A typhoon strikes the Korean peninsula flattening hundreds of houses and reportedly killing 2,000 people. |
| 20 | December 19 - Cunard announce that the luxury passenger ship RMS Aquitania, which made its maiden voyage in 1914, would be withdrawn from service. In early 1950 the ship sailed from Southampton to Faslane in Scotland where she was broken up. The scrapping took almost a year to complete and ended an illustrious career which included steaming 3 million miles on 450 voyages. Aquitania had carried 1.2 million passengers over a career that spanned nearly 36 years, making her the longest-serving Express Liner of the 20th century and the only major liner to serve in both World Wars. |

# 1949 INVENTIONS & DISCOVERIES

| | |
|---|---|
| 1 | Willard Libby and his colleagues at the University of Chicago discover a dating method that uses the naturally occurring radioisotope carbon-14 to determine the age of carbonaceous materials (radiocarbon dating). For his contributions to the team that developed this process, Libby was awarded the Nobel Prize in Chemistry in 1960. |
| 2 | American Gilmore Schjeldahl invents the airsickness bag. |
| 3 | Physicist Harold Lyons and his colleagues build the first atomic clock for the U.S. National Bureau of Standards. It was an ammonia maser device and although less accurate than existing quartz clocks it served to demonstrate the concept. The first accurate atomic clock, a caesium standard based on a certain transition of the caesium-133 atom, was built by Louis Essen and Jack Parry in 1955 at the National Physical Laboratory in the U.K. |
| 4 | Ed Seymour of Sycamore, Illinois invents aerosol spray paint. |
| 5 | Valerie Hunter Gordon is granted a U.K. patent for what is considered to be the world's first disposable nappy, the PADDI. In 1951 the PADDI patent was granted for the U.S. and worldwide. |

# U.S. PERSONALITIES
# BORN IN 1949

**George Edward Foreman**
January 10, 1949

Former professional boxer who competed from 1969 to 1977 and from 1987 to 1997. He is a two-time world heavyweight champion and an Olympic gold medalist. Outside the sport he is an ordained minister, author, and entrepreneur. Foreman remains the oldest world heavyweight champion in history and retired with a final record of 76 wins (68 knockouts) and 5 losses. Foreman has been inducted into both the World Boxing Hall of Fame and International Boxing Hall of Fame.

**Linda Susan Boreman**
January 10, 1949 - April 22, 2002

Pornographic actress commonly referred to by her onetime stage name Linda Lovelace. She is most famous for her performance in the 1972 hardcore porn film Deep Throat, which was an enormous success at the time. It was later alleged by Boreman that her abusive husband, Chuck Traynor, had threatened and coerced her into making the film. Boreman went on to become a born again Christian and a spokeswoman for the anti-pornography movement.

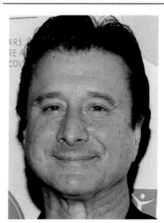

**Stephen Ray Perry**
January 22, 1949

Singer, songwriter, and record producer who is best known as the lead singer of the rock band Journey during their most commercially successful periods, from 1977 to 1987, and again from 1995 to 1998. Journey has sold over 75 million records worldwide making them one of the world's best-selling bands of all time. Perry has also had a successful solo career and was inducted into the Rock and Roll Hall of Fame as a member of Journey on April 7, 2017.

**John Adam Belushi**
January 24, 1949 -
March 5, 1982

Comedian, actor and singer. Belushi is best known for his 'intense energy and raucous attitude' which he displayed as one of the seven original cast members of the NBC sketch comedy show Saturday Night Live. Throughout his career Belushi had a close personal and artistic partnership with his fellow SNL star Dan Aykroyd. They made three movies together, most notably The Blues Brothers, which earned just under $5 million in its opening weekend and went on to gross $115.2 million in theaters worldwide.

**Gregg Charles Popovich**
January 28, 1949

Basketball coach who is currently the head coach of the San Antonio Spurs of the NBA. Taking over as coach of the Spurs in 1996, Popovich is the longest tenured active coach in the NBA and is considered one of the greatest coaches in NBA history. He is currently tied with Phil Jackson with a record 20 consecutive winning seasons, has won five NBA championships as a head coach, and is one of only nine coaches to have won 1,000 NBA games.

**Ivana Marie Trump**
February 20, 1949

Czech-American businesswoman and former fashion model who was the first wife of President Donald Trump (1977-1992). They have three children together, Donald Trump Jr., Ivanka Trump and Eric Trump. After her divorce she developed lines of clothing, fashion jewelry and beauty products that have been sold through television shopping channels. In 2017 she released an autobiography, Raising Trump, which covered her own upbringing and the early years of raising her children with Donald Trump.

**Richard Morgan Fliehr**, aka Ric Flair
February 25, 1949

Professional wrestling manager and retired professional wrestler signed to WWE under its Legends program. Widely regarded as the greatest professional wrestler of all time and the best American performer of the 1980s, he had a career that spanned 40 years. Flair is officially recognized by WWE and Pro Wrestling Illustrated (PWI) as a 16-time world champion. He was the first holder of the WCW World Heavyweight Championship and became the first person to complete WCW's Triple Crown.

**Cheryl Gates McFadden**
March 2, 1949

Actress and choreographer who is usually credited as Cheryl McFadden when working as a choreographer and Gates McFadden when working as an actress. She is best known for playing Dr. Beverly Crusher in the Star Trek: The Next Generation television series and in the four subsequent films. McFadden has taught at several universities including the American Academy of Dramatic Arts, Brandeis, Harvard, Purdue, Temple, the Stella Academy in Hamburg, and the University of Pittsburgh.

**Barbara Ann Corcoran**
March 10, 1949

Businesswoman, investor, speaker, consultant, syndicated columnist, author, and television personality. Corcoran has been an investor on ABC's three-time Emmy award winning show Shark Tank for nine seasons. She has made a total of 52 deals (including tandem ventures) on the show, the largest being with the company Coverplay for $350,000. Her average investment size is $103,113 and she has invested over $5.4 million to date.

**Patrick Duffy**
March 17, 1949

Actor, best known for his role on the CBS primetime soap opera Dallas where he played Bobby Ewing, the youngest son of Miss Ellie (Barbara Bel Geddes) and the brother of J.R. Ewing (Larry Hagman) in 326 episodes from 1978 to 1991. He is also well known for his role as Mark Harris on NBC's Man from Atlantis (1977-1978), Frank Lambert on the ABC sitcom Step by Step (1991-1998) and Stephen Logan on CBS's daytime soap opera The Bold and the Beautiful (2006-2011).

**Judith Arlene Resnik**
April 5, 1949 -
January 28, 1986

Engineer and a NASA astronaut who died when the Space Shuttle Challenger was destroyed during the launch of mission STS-51-L. Resnik was the second American female astronaut in space, logging 145 hours in orbit, and also the first Jewish woman of any nationality in space. She was a graduate of Carnegie Mellon University and had a Ph.D. in electrical engineering from the University of Maryland. The IEEE Judith Resnik Award for space engineering is named in her honor.

**Jessica Phyllis Lange**
April 20, 1949

Actress who has received worldwide acclaim for her work in film, theater, and television. She is the recipient of several awards, including two Academy Awards, one Tony Award, three Emmy Awards, five Golden Globe Awards, one Screen Actors Guild Award, and three Dorian Awards. In addition to acting Lange is a photographer with three published works and currently holds a Goodwill Ambassador position for UNICEF, specializing in HIV/AIDS in the Democratic Republic of the Congo and in Russia.

**John Harold Force**
May 4, 1949

NHRA drag racer who is a 16-time Funny Car champion driver and a 20-time champion car owner. Force owns and drives for John Force Racing. He is one of the most dominant drag racers in the sport with 144 career victories and became the first driver to set an official NHRA Funny Car elapsed time under five seconds in the quarter mile (October 16, 1993). He is the father of drag racers Ashley Force Hood, Brittany Force, and Courtney Force. His oldest daughter Adria Hight is the CFO of John Force Racing.

**William Martin 'Billy' Joel**
May 9, 1949

Singer-songwriter and pianist. Since releasing his first hit song Piano Man in 1973, Joel has become the sixth best-selling recording artist and the third best-selling solo artist in the United States. Joel had 33 Top 40 hits in the 1970s, 1980s and 1990s, all of which he wrote himself. He is also a six-time Grammy Award winner (with 23 nominations) and has been inducted into the Songwriters Hall of Fame (1992), the Rock and Roll Hall of Fame (1999), and the Long Island Music Hall of Fame (2006).

**Mary Pope Osborne**
May 20, 1949

Children's author whose best-known works include over forty books in her award-winning Magic Tree House series. The books have been translated into more than thirty languages and have sold more than 135 million copies worldwide. Osborne is an ardent advocate and supporter of children's literacy, and she has received honors from organizations such as the National Council of Teachers of English and the American Booksellers Association.

**Randall Hank Williams**
May 26, 1949

Singer-songwriter and musician, known professionally as Hank Williams Jr. Between 1979 and 1992, Williams released 21 albums that were all at least certified gold by the RIAA. He also enjoyed a string of 30 Top Ten singles on the Billboard Country charts which included eight No.1 singles. In 1987 and 1988, Williams was named Entertainer of the Year by the Country Music Association, and in 1987, 1988, and 1989, he won the same award from the Academy of Country Music.

**Lionel Brockman Richie Jr.**
June 20, 1949

Singer, songwriter, actor and record producer. In 1968 he started as a member of the funk and soul band the Commodores, and in 1982 went on to launch a solo career and became one of the most successful balladeers of the 1980s. Richie has sold over 90 million records worldwide, making him one of the world's best-selling artists of all time. He is also a five-time Grammy Award winner and in 2016 received the Songwriters Hall of Fame's highest honor, the Johnny Mercer Award.

**Mary Louise Streep**
June 22, 1949

Actress known professionally as Meryl Streep. She is cited in the media as the best actress of her generation and has been nominated for a record 21 Academy Awards (winning three). Streep has also received 31 Golden Globe nominations (winning eight) which is more nominations and competitive wins than any other actor. President Barack Obama awarded her the 2010 National Medal of Arts, and in 2014, the Presidential Medal of Freedom.

**Gene Klein**
August 25, 1949

Israeli-American musician, singer, songwriter, record producer, entrepreneur, actor and television personality, known professionally as Gene Simmons. He is the bassist and co-lead singer of Kiss, the rock band he co-founded with lead singer and rhythm guitarist Paul Stanley in the early 1970s. Kiss is one of the best-selling bands in the history of rock music having sold more than 75 million records worldwide. On April 10, 2014, Kiss was inducted into the Rock and Roll Hall of Fame.

**Richard Tiffany Gere**
August 31, 1949

Actor and humanitarian activist who started in films in the 1970s by playing a supporting role in Looking for Mr. Goodbar (1977), and a starring role in Days of Heaven (1978). He came to prominence though for his role in the film American Gigolo (1980), which established him as a leading man and a sex symbol. He went on to star in many well-received films, such as An Officer and a Gentleman (1982), The Cotton Club (1984), Pretty Woman (1990), Runaway Bride (1999), I'm Not There (2007) and Arbitrage (2012).

**Gloria Gaynor**
September 7, 1949

Singer best known for the disco era hits, I Will Survive, and Never Can Say Goodbye. I Will Survive was originally the B-side when Polydor Records released it in late 1978 but Boston Disco Radio DJ Jack King turned the record over and it became a monster hit. The song received the Grammy Award for Best Disco Recording in 1980, the only year that award was given, and in 2016 it was selected for induction into the Library of Congress' National Recording Registry.

**Bruce Frederick Joseph Springsteen**
September 23, 1949

Singer-songwriter known for his work with the E Street Band. Nicknamed 'The Boss', his most successful studio albums are Born to Run (1975) and Born in the U.S.A. (1984). Springsteen has sold more than 140 million records worldwide and has earned numerous awards for his work including 20 Grammy Awards, two Golden Globes, and an Academy Award. He has been inducted into both the Songwriters Hall of Fame and the Rock And Roll Hall Of Fame, and in 2016 was awarded the Presidential Medal of Freedom.

**Susan Alexandra Weaver**
October 8, 1949

Actress known professionally as Sigourney Weaver. Following her film debut as a minor character in Annie Hall (1977), she quickly came to prominence with her first lead role as Ellen Ripley in Alien (1979). She reprised the role in three sequels, including Aliens (1986), for which she was nominated for the Academy Award for Best Actress. She is also known for her roles in other box-office hits such as Ghostbusters (1984), Gorillas in the Mist (1988), Working Girl (1988), WALL-E (2008) and Avatar (2009).

**Caitlyn Marie Jenner**
October 28, 1949

Television personality and retired Olympic gold medal-winning decathlete formerly known as Bruce Jenner. Jenner won the 1976 Olympic decathlon event in Montreal, setting a third successive world record and gaining fame as an all-American hero. A career in television, film, writing, auto racing, business and as a Playgirl cover model followed. Since 2007 Jenner has appeared on the reality television series Keeping Up with the Kardashians and in 2015 revealed her identity as a transgender woman.

**James Vincent Young**
November 14, 1949

Guitarist, singer, and songwriter who is best known for playing lead guitar in the rock band Styx. In 1970 Young joined the band TW4 whilst a student at Illinois Institute of Technology, that band later became the first incarnation of Styx. Styx has had 4 consecutive albums certified multi-platinum by the RIAA, as well as 16 Top 40 singles in the U.S., 8 of which hit the Top 10. Some of the group's most popular songs include Lady, Come Sail Away, Babe, The Best of Times, and Mr. Roboto.

**Garry Emmanuel Shandling**
November 29, 1949 -
March 24, 2016

Comedian, actor, director, writer, producer and voice artist, best known for his work on It's Garry Shandling's Show and The Larry Sanders Show. He began his career writing for sitcoms such as Sanford and Son and Welcome Back, Kotter. During his three-decade career, Shandling was nominated for 19 Primetime Emmy Awards and two Golden Globe Awards, along with many other awards and nominations. He served as host of the Grammy Awards four times and as host of the Emmy Awards three times.

**Jeffrey Leon Bridges**
December 4, 1949

Actor, singer, and producer who won the 2009 Academy Award for Best Actor. Bridges has additionally been nominated for Academy Awards on six other occasions, including being one of the youngest actors ever (aged 22) when nominated for Best Supporting Actor in The Last Picture Show (1971). His only Oscar win came aged 60 for Crazy Heart (2009), making him one of the oldest ever winners of an Academy Award. Crazy Heart also brought him a Golden Globe and the Screen Actors Guild Award.

**Thomas Oliver 'Tom' Kite, Jr.**
December 9, 1949

Professional golfer and golf course architect who spent 175 weeks in the Top-10 of the Official World Golf Ranking between 1989 and 1994. He has 19 PGA Tour victories, including the 1992 U.S. Open at Pebble Beach. He has also competed on seven Ryder Cup squads (1979, 1981, 1983, 1985, 1987, 1989 and 1993) and served as the 1997 captain. In 1989 he was named PGA of America, Player of the Year, and he was inducted into the World Golf Hall of Fame in 2004.

**Randy Yeuell Owen**
December 13, 1949

Country music artist best known for his role as the lead singer of country rock band Alabama, which saw tremendous mainstream success throughout the 1980s and 1990s. Alabama are today the most successful band in the history of country music having released over 20 gold and platinum records, dozens of No.1 singles, and selling over 75 million records. They are also the most awarded band in the history of country music with over 200 awards from a variety of organizations.

**Donald Wayne 'Don' Johnson**
December 15, 1949

Actor, producer, director, singer, and songwriter. Johnson is probably best known for playing the role of James 'Sonny' Crockett in the 1980s television series Miami Vice (1984-1989) and had the eponymous lead role in the 1990s cop series Nash Bridges (1996-2001). Away from acting he released two pop music albums in the 1980s, from which his single Heartbeat reached No.5 on the Billboard Hot 100 singles chart. He was also the American Power Boat Association's 1988 World Powerboat Champion.

**Mary Elizabeth 'Sissy' Spacek**
December 25, 1949

Actress and singer who began her career in the early 1970s and first gained attention for her role in the film Badlands (1973). Her major breakthrough came in 1976 when she played the title character of Carrie White in Brian De Palma's horror film Carrie, which earned her an Oscar nomination. Spacek is a six-time Academy Award nominee, winning once for Coal Miner's Daughter (1980). She has also won three Golden Globe Awards for; Coal Miner's Daughter, Crimes of the Heart (1986) and In the Bedroom (2001).

# 1949 TOP 10 SINGLES

| | | |
|---|---|---|
| Vaughn Monroe | No.1 | Ghost Riders In The Sky |
| Frankie Laine | No.2 | That Lucky Old Sun |
| Vic Damone | No.3 | You're Breaking My Heart |
| Perry Como | No.4 | Some Enchanted Evening |
| Margaret Whiting & Jimmy Wakely | No.5 | Slipping Around |
| The Andrews Sisters | No.6 | I Can Dream, Can't I |
| Russ Morgan & His Orchestra | No.7 | Cruising Down The River |
| Evelyn Knight | No.8 | A Little Bird Told Me |
| Frankie Laine | No.9 | Mule Train |
| Al Morgan | No.10 | Jealous Heart |

# Vaughn Monroe
# Ghost Riders In The Sky

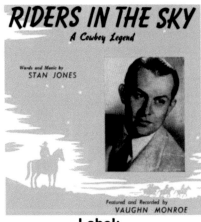

| Label: | Written by: | Length: |
|---|---|---|
| RCA Victor | Stan Jones | 2 mins 56 secs |

**Vaughn Wilton Monroe** (b. October 7, 1911 - d. May 21, 1973) was a baritone singer, trumpeter, big band leader and actor whose popularity was at its height in the 1940s and 1950s. Monroe formed his first orchestra in Boston in 1940 and became its principal vocalist. He has two stars on the Hollywood Walk of Fame one for recording and one for radio.

---

# Frankie Laine
# That Lucky Old Sun

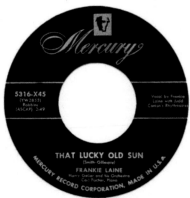

| Label: | Written by: | Length: |
|---|---|---|
| Mercury | Smith / Gillespie | 2 mins 49 secs |

**Frankie Laine** (b. Francesco Paolo LoVecchio; March 30, 1913 - d. February 6, 2007) was an American singer, songwriter and actor whose career spanned 75 years. His first concerts, with a marathon dance company, were in 1930 and his final performance was in 2005 with the song That's My Desire. This recording of 'That Lucky Old Sun' was released by Mercury Records and first reached the Billboard magazine Best Seller chart on August 19, 1949. It lasted a total of 22 weeks on the chart and peaked at No.1.

## ③ Vic Damone
## You're Breaking My Heart

| Label: | Written by: | Length: |
|---|---|---|
| Mercury | Genaro / Skylar | 2 mins 48 secs |

**Vic Damone** (b. Vito Rocco Farinola; June 12, 1928 - d. February 11, 2018) was an Italian American traditional pop and big band singer, songwriter, actor, radio and television presenter, and entertainer. He is best known for his performances of songs such as 'You're Breaking My Heart', 'On the Street Where You Live' (from My Fair Lady) and 'My Heart Cries for You'. Damone's 'You're Breaking My Heart' entered the Billboard chart on June 10, 1949, and peaked at No.1. Other less popular versions of this song by The Ink Spots, Buddy Clark, Jan Garber and Ralph Flanagan were also released in 1949.

---

## ④ Perry Como
## Some Enchanted Evening

| Label: | Written by: | Length: |
|---|---|---|
| RCA Victor | Rodgers / Hammerstein | 3 mins 35 secs |

**Pierino Ronald 'Perry' Como** (b. May 18, 1912 - d. May 12, 2001) was a singer and television personality. During a career spanning more than half a century he recorded exclusively for RCA Victor after signing with the label in 1943. 'Some Enchanted Evening' is a show tune from the Rodgers and Hammerstein musical South Pacific (1949), and is the single biggest popular hit to come out of any of their shows.

# Margaret Whiting & Jimmy Wakely
# Slipping Around

| Label: | Written by: | Length: |
|---|---|---|
| Capitol Records | Floyd Tillman | 2 mins 14 secs |

**Margaret Eleanor Whiting** (b. July 22, 1924 - d. January 10, 2011) was a singer whose career was at its peak during the 1940s and 1950s. **James Clarence Wakely** (b. February 16, 1914 - d. September 23, 1982) was an actor and one of the last singing cowboys. From 1949 through 1951 Whiting and Wakely's duets produced 9 top seven hits including their No.1 hit 'Slipping Around'.

---

# The Andrews Sisters
# I Can Dream, Can't I

| Label: | Written by: | Length: |
|---|---|---|
| Decca | Irving Kahal / Sammy Fain | 2 mins 36 secs |

**The Andrews Sisters** were a close harmony singing group from the eras of swing and boogie-woogie. The group consisted of three sisters: LaVerne Sophia (b. July 6, 1911 - d. May 8, 1967), Maxene Angelyn (b. January 3, 1916 - d. October 21, 1995) and Patricia Marie (b. February 16, 1918 - d. January 30, 2013). Throughout their long career the sisters sold well over 75 million records. Although the song 'I Can Dream, Can't I?' was first published in 1937, this version by the Andrews Sisters (and the Gordon Jenkins' orchestra) is the best known. It first reached the Billboard charts on September 16, 1949, and made it to No.1 on all three of the magazine's main pop charts (Best Sellers in Stores, Most Played by Jockeys, and Most Played in Jukeboxes).

### 7 Russ Morgan & His Orchestra
### Cruising Down The River

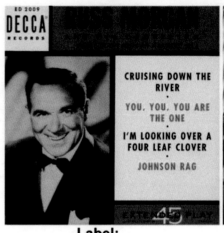

| Label: | Written by: | Length: |
| --- | --- | --- |
| Decca | Beadell / Tollerton | 2 mins 33 secs |

**Russ Morgan** (b. April 29, 1904 - d. August 7, 1969) was a big band orchestra leader and musical arranger during the 1930s and 1940s. In 1949, four songs he recorded made it big on the charts, So Tired, Cruising Down The River, Sunflower, and Forever And Ever. The song 'Cruising Down The River' was written by two middle-aged women (Eily Beadell and Nell Tollerton) as part of a public song writing competition held in the UK in 1945. It was one of the biggest hits of Morgan's career.

---

### 8 Evelyn Knight
### A Little Bird Told Me

| Label: | Written by: | Length: |
| --- | --- | --- |
| Decca | Harvey Brooks | 2 mins 41 secs |

**Evelyn Knight** (b. December 31, 1917 - d. September 28, 2007) was an American singer who, during a seven-year span in the late 1940s and early 1950s, had two No.1 hit records and 13 that made the Top 40. 'A Little Bird Told Me' (performed with The Stardusters) was her first No.1 record and spent 7 weeks in the top spot. The flip side to the single 'Brush Those Tears From Your Eyes' also charted, peaking at No.24.

**⑨ Frankie Laine
Mule Train**

| **Label:** | **Written by:** | **Length:** |
|---|---|---|
| Mercury | Glickman / Heath / Lange | 2 mins 30 secs |

The **Frankie Laine** recording of 'Mule Train' first reached the Billboard magazine charts on November 4, 1949 where it stayed for 13 weeks, peaking at No.1. The song featured a bellowed vocal delivery and studio-created gimmicks such as whip-cracking sound effects. It is often cited as an outstanding early example of studio production techniques. Other recordings of 'Mule Train' include Vaughn Monroe's version in the Western, Singing Guns (1950), which was nominated for the Academy Award for Best Original Song but lost out to the song 'Mona Lisa'.

---

**⑩ Al Morgan
Jealous Heart**

| **Label:** | **Written by:** | **Length:** |
|---|---|---|
| London Records | Jenny Lou Carson | 2 mins 11 secs |

**Al 'Flying Fingers' Morgan** (b. November 14, 1915 - d. November 18, 1989) was a popular nightclub singer, pianist and composer who is known for his hit recordings Jealous Heart, I'll Take Care Of Your Cares, and The Place Where I Worship. Morgan was also one of the first musicians to have his own syndicated television show. 'Jealous Heart' was released in September 1949 and was his biggest hit. It stayed in the charts for six months and spent ten weeks in the Top 5.

# 1949: TOP FILMS

1. **Samson And Delilah** - *Paramount*
2. **Jolson Sings Again** - *Columbia*
3. **Sands Of Iwo Jima** - *Republic*
4. **Battleground** - *MGM*
5. **I Was A Male War Bride** - *20th Century Fox*

# OSCARS

**Best Picture:** All The King's Men

**Best Director:** Joseph L. Mankiewicz *(A Letter To Three Wives)*

| **Best Actor:** | **Best Actress:** |
| --- | --- |
| Broderick Crawford *(All The King's Men)* | Olivia de Havilland *(The Heiress)* |
| **Best Supporting Actor:** | **Best Supporting Actress:** |
| Dean Jagger *(Twelve O'Clock High)* | Mercedes McCambridge *(All The King's Men)* |

# SAMSON AND DELILAH

**Directed by: Cecil B. DeMille - Runtime: 2 hours 11 minutes**

The biblical story of strongman Samson and his love for Delilah, the woman who seduces him, discovers the secret of his strength, and then betrays him to the Philistines.

# STARRING

**Hedy Lamarr**
Born: November 9, 1914
Died: January 19, 2000

**Character:**
Delilah

Austrian-born American film actress and inventor, born Hedwig Eva Maria Kiesler. After a brief film career in Czechoslovakia, which included the controversial film Ecstasy (1933), she met MGM studio head Louis B. Mayer in Paris whilst he was scouting for talent in Europe. He offered her a movie contract in Hollywood and she became a film star from the late 1930s to the 1950s. Lamarr's biggest success was with her portrayal of Delilah in Samson and Delilah.

**Victor John Mature**
Born: January 29, 1913
Died: August 4, 1999

**Character:**
Samson

American stage, film, and television actor who starred most notably in several Biblical movies during the 1950s, and was known for his dark good looks and mega-watt smile. His best known film roles include One Million B.C. (1940), My Darling Clementine (1946), Kiss Of Death (1947), Samson And Delilah, and The Robe (1953). He also appeared in a large number of musicals opposite such stars as Rita Hayworth and Betty Grable.

**George Henry Sanders**
Born: July 3, 1906
Died: April 25, 1972

**Character:**
The Saran of Gaza

Russian-born English film and television actor, singer-songwriter, music composer, and author. His career as an actor spanned more than 40 years and he was often cast as sophisticated but villainous characters. He is perhaps best known for his roles as Jack Favell in Rebecca (1940), Addison DeWitt in All About Eve (1950), for which he won an Academy Award, and as Simon Templar, 'The Saint', in five films made in the 1930s and 1940s.

# TRIVIA

| | |
|---|---|
| **Goofs** | In the final destruction-of-the-temple scene, the huge statue of Dagon starts to topple head first, but in later shots it is seen sliding towards the camera feet first. This is because director Cecil DeMille was not satisfied with the first take and had the temple re-erected then collapsed a second time. Shots from both destructions were spliced together to make an exciting but rather puzzling final sequence. |
| **Interesting Facts** | Victor Mature won the role of Samson over Burt Lancaster. Lancaster was suffering from a back injury at the time and was ultimately considered too young for the part. |

# CONTINUED

**Interesting Facts**
With Samson And Delilah grossing $28 million domestically in the United States, it became Paramount's biggest hit since DeMille's silent version of The Ten Commandments (1923).

For the scene in which Samson kills the lion, Victor Mature refused to wrestle a tame movie lion. Told by director Cecil B. DeMille that the lion had no teeth, Mature replied, "I don't want to be gummed to death, either." The scene shows a stunt man wrestling the tame lion, intercut with close-ups of Mature wrestling a lion skin.

Much discussion took place during the shooting of the scene where Samson kisses Delilah as to whether a man kisses a woman with his eyes closed or open. Victor Mature insisted that a fellow would be a chump to close his eyes when kissing Hedy Lamarr. In the final shot, Mature closed, opened, and then closed his eyes again.

Of Samson And Delilah's five Academy Award nominations the film won two, for Best Art Direction and Best Costume Design.

At the premiere, Cecil B. DeMille asked Groucho Marx what he thought of the film. Groucho replied, "Well, there's just one problem, C.B. No picture can hold my interest where the leading man's tits are bigger than the leading lady's." DeMille was not amused, by Marx's remark, but Victor Mature apparently was.

**Quotes**
**Prince Ahtur:** This Samson has some unknown power, some secret that gives him superhuman strength. No man can stand against him.
**Delilah:** Perhaps he'll fall before a woman. Even Samson's strength must have a weakness. There isn't a man in the world who would not share his secrets with some woman.

**Samson:** You came to this house as wedding guests. Fire and death are your gifts to my bride. For all that I do against you now, I shall be blameless. I'll give you back fire for fire, and death for death!

# JOLSON SINGS AGAIN

**Directed by: Henry Levin - Runtime: 1 hour 36 minutes**

In this sequel to The Jolson Story (1946), we pick up the singer's career just as he has returned to the stage after a premature retirement.

# STARRING

**Larry Parks**
Born: December 13, 1914
Died: April 13, 1975

**Character:**
Al Jolson / Larry Parks

Stage and movie actor born Samuel Klausman Lawrence Parks. His career arced from bit player and supporting roles to top billing, before his career was virtually ended when he admitted to having once been a member of a Communist party cell (this led to him being blacklisted by all Hollywood studios). His best known role was as Al Jolson, whom he portrayed in two films: The Jolson Story (1946) and Jolson Sings Again.

**Barbara Hale**
Born: April 18, 1922
Died: January 26, 2017

**Character:**
Ellen Clark

Actress best known for her role as legal secretary Della Street on more than 270 episodes of the Perry Mason television series (1957-1966), which earned her the 1959 Emmy Award for Outstanding Supporting Actress in a Drama Series. She reprised the role in 30 Perry Mason movies for television. Her most notable film roles include Higher And Higher (1943), West Of The Pecos (1945), Lady Luck (1946), The Window (1949) and Jolson Sings Again.

**William Demarest**
Born: February 27, 1892
Died: December 27, 1983

**Character:**
Steve Martin

Character actor popularly known for playing Uncle Charley in the ABC / CBS sitcom My Three Sons (1965-1972). A veteran of World War I, he became a prolific film and television actor. Demarest appeared in over 140 films throughout his career and received an Academy Award nomination during this time for his supporting role in The Jolson Story (1946). He had previously shared the screen with the real Al Jolson in The Jazz Singer (1927).

# TRIVIA

**Interesting Facts**

After appearing as himself in a long shot of 'Swanee' (uncredited) in The Jolson Story (1946), Al Jolson had wanted to make an appearance as himself in this film too. Although he didn't actually get to play himself, he does appear. During the filming of 'The Jolson Story' the man standing watching the filming in a gray cowboy hat is Jolson.

The film was nominated for three Academy Awards: Cinematography (Color), Music (Scoring of a Musical Picture) and Writing (Story and Screenplay).

# CONTINUED

|  |  |
|---|---|
| **Interesting Facts** | 'Lux Radio Theater' broadcast a 60-minute radio adaptation of the movie on May 22, 1950, with Barbara Hale and William Demarest reprising their film roles. Al Jolson, who provides the singing for Larry Parks in the film, plays himself. |
|  | According to an interview with Ray Henderson, one of the composers of 'Sonny Boy', the song was written as a satire. They were tired of Al Jolson's Mammy-type songs and wanted to write one so syrupy and sentimental that he wouldn't sing it. He heard it, loved it, changed a few of the lyrics and made it his signature tune. |
|  | For the film Al Jolson auditioned to play himself. |
|  | In this sequel, the story reaches the point in Jolson's life where a film of his life is to be made (first film: The Jolson Story), and in preparation for the film Jolson meets the actor who is to portray him. In what is probably a cinema first, Parks plays both Jolson and himself (the young Larry Parks) as they meet in a split-screen scene. |
| **Quote** | **Ellen Clark**: *[leaving room]*<br>My! We'll soon be smart as pigs! |

# SANDS OF IWO JIMA

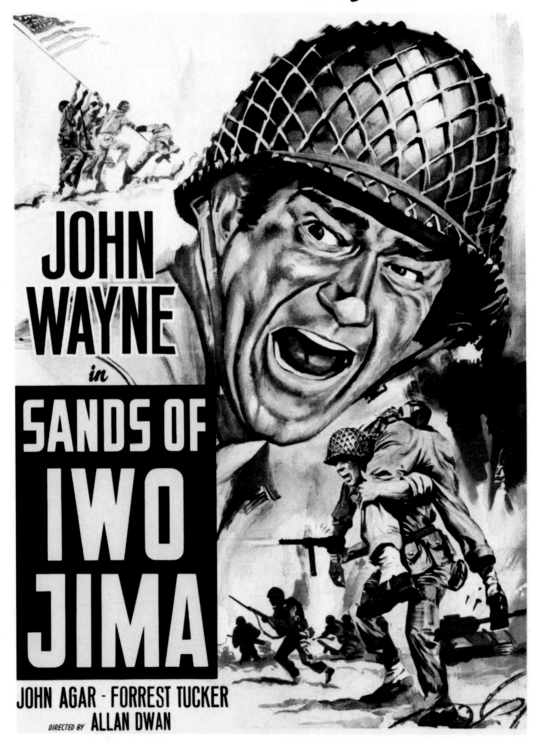

**Directed by: Allan Dwan - Runtime: 1 hour 40 minutes**

After his wife takes their son and leaves him, Sgt. John Stryker is an embittered man who takes his misery out a bunch of green recruits who have a hard time dealing with his tough drills and thick skin. In the end, as survival in the bloody battle of Iwo Jima depends on the lessons he has taught them, his troops discover why he was so tough.

# STARRING

**John Wayne**
Born: May 26, 1907
Died: June 11, 1979

**Character:**
Sgt. John M. Stryker

Actor, director and producer who was born Marion Robert Morrison. Nicknamed Duke, his career took off in 1939 with John Ford's Stagecoach making him an instant star. Wayne went on to feature in a further 141 pictures and was nominated for an Academy Award on three occasions, winning once for Best Actor in True Grit (1969). He was posthumously awarded the Presidential Medal of Freedom on the 9th June 1980.

**John George Agar, Jr.**
Born: January 31, 1921
Died: April 7, 2002

**Characters:**
PFC Peter Conway

Actor best known for starring alongside John Wayne in the films Sands Of Iwo Jima, Fort Apache (1948), and She Wore A Yellow Ribbon (1949). In his later career he developed a niche playing leading men in low-budget science fiction, Western, and horror movies. He was the star of B movies such as Tarantula (1955), The Mole People (1956), and The Brain From Planet Arous (1957). Agar was married to Shirley Temple for 5 years until their divorce in 1950.

**Adele Mara**
Born: April 28, 1923
Died: May 7, 2010

**Character:**
Allison Bromley

Spanish-American actress, singer, and dancer born Adelaida Delgado. She started her career aged 15 as a singer/dancer with Xavier Cugat and His Orchestra in Detroit. Cugat took her to New York where she was spotted by a Columbia talent scout. Mara appeared in many films during the 1940s and 1950s, and was also a popular pinup girl. Her career continued on television in the 1950s and 1960s, and she featured in a number of guest roles, primarily in westerns.

# TRIVIA

| | |
|---|---|
| **Goofs** | In the training scenes, set in New Zealand, a row of Eucalyptus trees are seen. These are native to Australia and are not found in New Zealand. |
| | Near the beginning of the film, while the platoon is marching and Conway is talking about his Father, his helmet strap keeps switching from swinging lose to being tucked under his rifle strap. |
| **Interesting Facts** | Kirk Douglas was considered for the role of Sgt. Stryker before director Allan Dwan realized he could get John Wayne to play the part. |

# CONTINUED

**Interesting Facts** | This film recreates the famous 'Raising Of The Flag' photograph taken on Iwo Jima by Joe Rosenthal on February 23, 1945. The three surviving flag raisers from that day make a cameo appearance during this scene. Rene A. Gagnon, Ira H. Hayes and John H. Bradley are seen with John Wayne as he instructs them to hoist the flag. The flag used to recreate the incident is the actual flag that was raised on Mount Suribachi and was loaned to the movie by the U.S. Marine Corps Museum.

At $1.4 million this was the most expensive movie Republic Pictures had ever made. It went on to gross $13.9 million.

Sands Of Iwo Jima gave John Wayne his first ever Academy Award nomination for Best Actor (won by Broderick Crawford in 'All The King's Men'). Wayne wouldn't be nominated again for 20 years until True Grit (1969), when he would win the Best Actor Award for playing Reuben J. 'Rooster' Cogburn.

**Quotes** | **Sgt. Stryker:** You gotta learn right and you gotta learn fast. And any man that doesn't want to cooperate, I'll make him wish he had never been born.

**PFC. Al Thomas:** I got a great future, for the next couple of hours.

# BATTLEGROUND

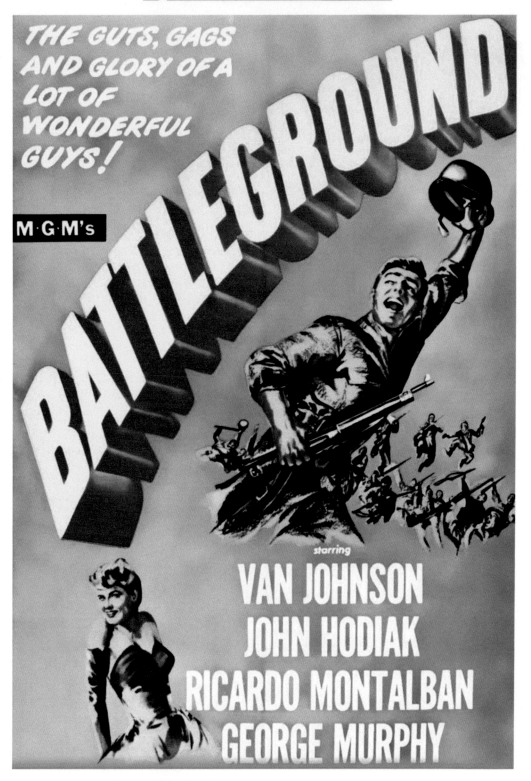

**Directed by: William A. Wellman - Runtime: 1 hour 58 minutes**

A squad of the 101st Airborne Division copes with being trapped in the besieged city of Bastogne during the Battle of the Bulge.

# STARRING

**Van Johnson**
Born: August 25, 1916
Died: December 12, 2008

**Character:**
Holley

Film/television actor and dancer who was a major star at Metro-Goldwyn-Mayer during and after World War II. Born Charles Van Dell it was his embodiment of the boy-next-door wholesomeness that made him a popular Hollywood star in the 1940s and 1950s. Johnson's big break was in A Guy Named Joe (1943), starring Spencer Tracy and Irene Dunne. In 1945, Johnson tied with Bing Crosby as the top box office star chosen by the National Association of Theater Owners.

**John Hodiak**
Born: April 16, 1914
Died: October 19, 1955

**Character:**
Jarvess

American actor of Ukrainian and Polish descent who worked in radio, stage and film. Hodiak arrived in Hollywood in 1942 and signed a motion picture contract with MGM. Hodiak first came to notice in Alfred Hitchcock's classic Lifeboat (1944) and followed this with equally fine performances in A Bell For Adano (1945) and Somewhere In The Night (1946). Perhaps his best known credit was as Judy Garland's leading man in The Harvey Girls (1946).

**Ricardo Montalban**
Born: November 25, 1920
Died: January 14, 2009

**Character:**
Roderigues

Mexican actor (born Ricardo Gonzalo Pedro Montalbán y Merino) whose career spanned seven decades. Among his notable roles were Armando in the Planet Of The Apes film series and Khan Noonien Singh in the film Star Trek II: The Wrath of Khan (1982). His best-known television roles were that of Mr Roarke on the television series Fantasy Island (1977-1984), his Emmy Award winning role in How the West Was Won (1976) and as a villain in the The Colbys (1985-1987).

# TRIVIA

| | |
|---|---|
| **Goofs** | When Holley hears Denise and Jarvess talking on the other side of the living room door he rushes into the corridor with a full cup of coffee. He takes one small sip and then puts, what is now an empty cup, in to his pocket. |
| | When the C-47s are dropping supplies to the soldiers, one of the stock footage pieces used shows paratroopers jumping from planes, not supplies being dropped. |
| **Interesting Facts** | Twenty veterans of the 101st Airborne who fought in the Bastogne area were hired to train the actors and were also used as extras. |

# CONTINUED

**Interesting Facts**

James Whitmore took over the role of Sergeant Kinnie after James Mitchell was fired for moving too much like a dancer and not enough like a drill sergeant.

James Arness (Garby) served in World War II and is the most decorated of the actors in the film. He received the Bronze Star, the Purple Heart, the European-African-Middle Eastern Campaign Medal with three bronze campaign stars, the World War II Victory Medal, and the Combat Infantryman Badge for his service.

Douglas Fowley (Private Kippton - who continually loses his false teeth) served in the Navy in the South Pacific in World War II, and lost all of his own teeth in an explosion aboard his aircraft carrier during battle.

A private showing of the film for President Harry S. Truman was arranged (even before the premiere in Washington, D.C. on the 9th November 1949) which was attended by Brigadier General Anthony McAuliffe who had commanded the 101st during the siege.

Battleground was MGM's largest grossing film in five years and was nominated for 6 Academy Awards, winning two for; Best Writing, Story and Screenplay, and Best Cinematography, (Black-and-White).

**Quote**

*[as Bettis is digging a foxhole]*
**Holley:** Let's not try to reach China this time, hey Bettis?
**Bettis:** Well there's no sense digging if you don't go deep.
**Holley:** The last one we dug one together, you went so deep that when I climbed out in the morning I got the bends.

# I WAS A MALE WAR BRIDE

**Directed by: Howard Hawks - Runtime: 1 hour 45 minutes**

After marrying American Lieutenant Catherine Gates, with whom he was assigned to work in post-war Germany, French Captain Henri Rochard tries to return to America under the auspices of America's 1945 War Brides Act.

# STARRING

**Cary Grant**
Born: January 18, 1904
Died: November 29, 1986

**Character:**
Capt. Henri Rochard

British-American actor (born Archibald Alec Leach) who is best known as one of classic Hollywood's definitive leading men. He began a career in Hollywood in the early 1930s and became known for his transatlantic accent, light-hearted approach to acting, comic timing and debonair demeanour. He was twice nominated for the Academy Award for Best Actor for his roles in; Penny Serenade (1941) and None But The Lonely Heart (1944).

**Clara Lou 'Ann' Sheridan**
Born: February 21, 1915
Died: January 21, 1967

**Character:**
Lt. Catherine Gates

Actress and singer who made an uncredited film debut aged 19 in Search For Beauty (1934). She worked regularly from 1934 to her death in 1967, first in film and later in television. Notable film roles include Angels With Dirty Faces (1938), The Man Who Came To Dinner (1942), Kings Row (1942), Nora Prentiss (1947) and I Was A Male War Bride. In television she starred in the soap opera Another World (1964) and the Western series Pistols 'n' Petticoats (1966).

**Marion Marshall**
Born: June 8, 1929

**Characters:**
Lt. Kitty Lawrence

Retired actress born Marian Lepriel Tanner. Her first film appearances were in the 20th Century Fox films Gentleman's Agreement and Daisy Kenyon in 1947 (both uncredited). She went on to play roles (many minor) in over 25 more films until 1967. Marshall had a small but significant role in I Was A Male War Bride and featured prominently in three Dean Martin and Jerry Lewis comedy films, That's My Boy (1951) The Stooge (1952), and Sailor Beware (1952).

# TRIVIA

**Goofs** | When Catherine and Henri come up to the dam, Henri is rowing. He jumps to the front of the boat to look over the edge. When he does so he drops the starboard oar into the water. The next scene shows him looking over the edge and when the camera cuts back to the aerial view you can see that both oars are now on the boat.

**Interesting Facts** | Eleanor Audley, whose voice was used to dub the assignment officer, was also the voice of some of Disney's greatest villains; Lady Tremaine the evil stepmother from Cinderella (1950), and the evil fairy, Maleficent, from Sleeping Beauty (1959).

# CONTINUED

**Interesting Facts**  Howard Hawks was given license to cast whomever he wanted in the supporting roles, so he cast his current girlfriend, Marion Marshall, in the role of Lt. Kitty Lawrence.

This was Howard Hawks' first film to be shot in Europe and it was beset with problems. The German winter was unbearably cold and most of the cast and crew fell ill. Ann Sheridan caught pleurisy (which developed into pneumonia), Cary Grant contracted hepatitis with jaundice, and Hawks broke out in hives. Due to the various illnesses of cast members the delay in production pushed the films budget to over $2 million.

**Quote**  **Soldier:** You're not Mrs. Rochard!
**Capt. Henri Rochard:** I'm MISTER Rochard.
**Soldier:** Well, it's your WIFE who must report here for transportation to Bremerhaven.
**Capt. Henri Rochard:** According to the War Department, I AM my wife.
**Soldier:** You can't be your wife!
**Capt. Henri Rochard:** If the American army says that I CAN be my wife, who am I to dispute them?

# SPORTING WINNERS

## LEON HART - COLLEGE FOOTBALL

**AP** Associated Press - MALE ATHLETE OF THE YEAR

**Leon Joseph Hart**
Born: November 2, 1928 in Pittsburgh, Pennsylvania
Died: September 24, 2002 in South Bend, Indiana
NFL Career: Detroit Lions (1950-1957)

Leon Hart was an American football end who won the Heisman Trophy and the Maxwell Award while at the University of Notre Dame in 1949. He went on to play in the NFL for eight seasons, from 1950 through 1957, with the Detroit Lions.

### Career Highlights

| | |
|---|---|
| Consensus National Champion | 1946, 1947, 1949 |
| All-American | 1948, 1949 |
| Heisman Trophy | 1949 |
| Maxwell Award | 1949 |
| Sporting News Player Of The Year | 1949 |
| AP Male Athlete Of The Year | 1949 |
| First-Team All-Pro | 1951 |
| Pro Bowl | 1951 |
| NFL Champion | 1952, 1953, 1957 |

Hart is the only lineman to win three college football national championships, three NFL Championships, and is the last of only two linemen ever to win the Heisman Trophy. He is also one of only three players, along with Angelo Bertelli and Cam Newton, to win the Heisman Trophy, a national championship, and be the first overall pick in the NFL draft all in the same one-year span. Hart was inducted into the College Football Hall of Fame in 1973.

# MARLENE BAUER - GOLF

## AP Associated Press - FEMALE ATHLETE OF THE YEAR

**Marlene Bauer Hagge**
Born: February 16, 1934 in Eureka, South Dakota
Professional Golf Career: 1950-1996

Marlene Bauer (better known today by her married name, Marlene Bauer Hagge) started playing golf at age 3 and by the age of 13 had won the Western and National Junior Championships, the Los Angeles Women's City Championship, the Palm Springs Women's Championship, Northern California Open and the Indio Women's Invitational. 1947 also saw her become the youngest player to make the cut at the U.S. Women's Open, finishing eighth. In 1949, at the age of 15, she became the youngest athlete ever to be named Associated Press Athlete of the Year, Golfer of the Year, and Teenager of the Year, and won the U.S. Girls' Junior and the WWGA Junior titles.

**Achievements & Awards:**

| | |
|---|---|
| Associated Press - Female Athlete Of The Year | 1949 |
| Women's PGA Championship | 1956 |
| LPGA Tour Money Winner | 1956 |
| Commissioner's Award (LPGA Founders) | 2000 |
| LPGA Tour Hall Of Fame | 2002 |
| World Golf Hall of Fame | 2002 |

Bauer was the youngest of the thirteen women who founded the LPGA in 1950, and remains the youngest ever member of the LPGA Tour. She won one major championship and 26 LPGA Tour events throughout her professional career, and in 2002 she was officially inducted into the World Golf Hall of Fame.

# GOLF

## THE MASTERS - SAM SNEAD

The Masters Tournament is the first of the majors to be played each year and unlike the other major championships it is played at the same location - Augusta National Golf Club, Georgia. This was the 13th Masters Tournament and was held April 7-10. Sam Snead shot consecutive rounds of 67 on the weekend to win by three strokes and take the first of his three Masters victories, and the third of his seven major championships. The total prize fund was $11,000 with $2,750 going to the winner. The 1949 Masters is noted as the first year that the famous Green Jacket was awarded to the tournament winner; previous champions were awarded theirs retroactively.

## PGA CHAMPIONSHIP - SAM SNEAD

The 1949 and 31st PGA Championship was played May 25-31 at Hermitage Country Club, northwest of Richmond, Virginia. Native Virginian Sam Snead won the match play championship, 3 & 2 over Johnny Palmer in the Tuesday final. The winner's share of the $17,700 prize fund was $3,500 with the runner-up receiving $1,500.

## U.S. OPEN - CARY MIDDLECOFF

The 1949 U.S. Open Championship (established in 1895) was held June 9-11 at Medinah Country Club in Medinah, Illinois, a suburb northwest of Chicago. Cary Middlecoff, a dentist, won the first of his two U.S. Open titles one stroke ahead of runners-up Clayton Heafner and Sam Snead. The total prize fund was $10,000 with Middlecoff taking home $2,000.

Sam Snead

Cary Middlecoff (left) & Sam Snead

# WORLD SERIES - NEW YORK YANKEES

**New York Yankees**     4 - 1     **Brooklyn Dodgers**

Total attendance: 236,710 - Average attendance: 47,342
Winning player's share: $5,627 - Losing player's share: $4,273

The World Series is the annual championship series of Major League Baseball. Played since 1903 between the American League (AL) champion team and the National League (NL) champion, it is determined through a best-of-seven playoff.

The 1949 World Series matched the New York Yankees against the Brooklyn Dodgers. The Yankees won in five games for their second defeat of the Dodgers in three years, and the twelfth championship in the teams history. This victory would start a record run of five consecutive World Series championships by the Yankees, and a run of 14 American League Pennants in 16 years (1949-1964 except for 1954 and 1959).

Both the New York Yankees and Brooklyn Dodgers finished the regular season with exactly the same records (including that of winning their respective leagues by exactly one game).

|   | Date | Score | | | Location | Time | Att. |
|---|------|-------|---|---|----------|------|------|
| 1 | Oct 5 | Dodgers | 0-1 | **Yankees** | Yankee Stadium | 2:24 | 66,224 |
| 2 | Oct 6 | **Dodgers** | 1-0 | Yankees | Yankee Stadium | 2:30 | 70,053 |
| 3 | Oct 7 | **Yankees** | 4-3 | Dodgers | Ebbets Field | 2:30 | 32,788 |
| 4 | Oct 8 | **Yankees** | 6-4 | Dodgers | Ebbets Field | 2:42 | 33,934 |
| 5 | Oct 9 | **Yankees** | 10-6 | Dodgers | Ebbets Field | 3:04 | 33,711 |

# HORSE RACING

Capot and jockey Ted Atkinson shortly after winning the 1949 Belmont Stakes.

Capot (1946-1974) was an American Thoroughbred racehorse owned and bred by Greentree Stable in Red Bank, New Jersey, and trained by John M. Gaver, Sr. By the end of his three-year-old season in 1949 Capot had won two of the three Triple Crown races, the Preakness Stakes and Belmont Stakes. In the Kentucky Derby he charged to the front of the field on the backstretch but was unable to withstand the rush from winner Ponder, and finished second. His performances earned him 1949's Three-Year-Old Male Champion honors and he was also named the 1949 Horse of the Year by the Daily Racing Form.

## KENTUCKY DERBY - PONDER

The Kentucky Derby is held annually at Churchill Downs in Louisville, Kentucky on the first Saturday in May. The race is a Grade 1 stakes race for three-year-olds and is one and a quarter miles in length.

## PREAKNESS STAKES - CAPOT

The Preakness Stakes is held on the third Saturday in May each year at Pimlico Race Course in Baltimore, Maryland. It is a Grade 1 race run over a distance of 9.5 furlongs (1 3/16 miles) on dirt.

## BELMONT STAKES - CAPOT

The Belmont Stakes is Grade 1 race held every June at Belmont Park in Elmont, New York. It is 1.5 miles in length and open to three-year-old thoroughbreds. It takes place on a Saturday between June 5 and June 11.

# FOOTBALL - NFL CHAMPIONSHIP

## CHAMPIONSHIP GAME

**Philadelphia Eagles**     **14 - 0**     **Los Angeles Rams**

Played: December 18, 1949 at Los Angeles Memorial Coliseum, California.
Attendance: 27,980 (paid), 22,245 (actual)
Winning player's share: $1,090 - Losing player's share: $789

The 1949 National Football League Championship Game was the 17th title game for the National Football League, and featured the Eastern Division champion Philadelphia Eagles (the defending NFL champions) against the Los Angeles Rams (winners of the Western Division). It is remembered for the driving rain that caused the field to become a mud pit; its paid attendance was 27,980 but only 22,245 made it to the stadium.

**Division Results:**

### Eastern Division

| Team | P | W | L | T | PCT | PF | PA |
|---|---|---|---|---|---|---|---|
| **Philadelphia Eagles** | **12** | **11** | **1** | **0** | **.917** | **364** | **134** |
| Pittsburgh Steelers | 12 | 6 | 5 | 1 | .545 | 224 | 214 |
| New York Giants | 12 | 6 | 6 | 0 | .500 | 287 | 298 |
| Washington Redskins | 12 | 4 | 7 | 1 | .364 | 268 | 339 |
| New York Bulldogs | 12 | 1 | 10 | 1 | .091 | 153 | 368 |

### Western Division

| Team | P | W | L | T | PCT | PF | PA |
|---|---|---|---|---|---|---|---|
| **Los Angeles Rams** | **12** | **8** | **2** | **2** | **.800** | **360** | **239** |
| Chicago Bears | 12 | 9 | 3 | 0 | .750 | 332 | 218 |
| Chicago Cardinals | 12 | 6 | 5 | 1 | .545 | 360 | 301 |
| Detroit Lions | 12 | 4 | 8 | 0 | .333 | 237 | 259 |
| Green Bay Packers | 12 | 2 | 10 | 0 | .167 | 114 | 329 |

P= Games Played, W = Wins, L = Losses, T = Ties,
PCT= Winning Percentage, PF= Points For, PA = Points Against
Note: The NFL did not officially count tie games in the standings until 1972.

### League Leaders

| Statistic | Name | Team | Yards |
|---|---|---|---|
| Passing | Johnny Lujack | Chicago Bears | 2658 |
| Rushing | Steve Van Buren | Philadelphia Eagles | 1146 |
| Receiving | Bob Mann | Detroit Lions | 1014 |

# HOCKEY: 1948-49 NHL SEASON

The 1948-49 NHL season was the 32nd season of the National Hockey League and included six teams each playing 60 games. The Toronto Maple Leafs were the Stanley Cup winners defeating the Detroit Red Wings 4-0 in a rematch of the previous seasons finals.

**Final Standings:**

| | Team | GP | W | L | T | GF | GA | Pts |
|---|---|---|---|---|---|---|---|---|
| 1 | **Detroit Red Wings** | 60 | 34 | 19 | 7 | 195 | 145 | 75 |
| 2 | Boston Bruins | 60 | 29 | 23 | 8 | 178 | 163 | 66 |
| 3 | Montreal Canadiens | 60 | 28 | 23 | 9 | 152 | 126 | 65 |
| 4 | Toronto Maple Leafs | 60 | 22 | 25 | 13 | 147 | 161 | 57 |
| 5 | Chicago Black Hawks | 60 | 21 | 31 | 8 | 173 | 211 | 50 |
| 6 | New York Rangers | 60 | 18 | 31 | 11 | 133 | 172 | 47 |

**Scoring Leaders:**

| | Player | Team | Goals | Assists | Points |
|---|---|---|---|---|---|
| 1 | **Roy Conacher** | **Chicago Black Hawks** | 26 | 42 | 68 |
| 2 | Doug Bentley | Chicago Black Hawks | 23 | 43 | 66 |
| 3 | Sid Abel | Detroit Red Wings | 28 | 26 | 54 |

Hart Trophy (Most Valuable Player): Sid Abel - Detroit Red Wings
Vezina Trophy (Fewest Goals Allowed): Bill Durnan - Montreal Canadiens

# STANLEY CUP

4 - 0

**Toronto Maple Leafs**                    **Detroit Red Wings**

**Series Summary:**

| | Date | Home Team | Result | Road Team |
|---|---|---|---|---|
| 1 | April 8 | **Toronto Maple Leafs** | 3-2 | Detroit Red Wings |
| 2 | April 10 | **Toronto Maple Leafs** | 3-1 | Detroit Red Wings |
| 3 | April 13 | Detroit Red Wings | 1-3 | **Toronto Maple Leafs** |
| 4 | April 16 | Detroit Red Wings | 1-3 | **Toronto Maple Leafs** |

# INDIANAPOLIS 500 - BILL HOLLAND

Bill Holland wins the 1949 Indy 500 in a Lou Moore, Blue Crown Spark Plug Spl.

The 33rd International 500-Mile Sweepstakes Race was held at the Indianapolis Motor Speedway on Monday, May 30, 1949. The race was won by Bill Holland in front of a crowd of 150,000 spectators - he had come second in both 1947 and 1948. Driving for Lou Moore, Holland completed the race with an average speed of 121.327mph.

Late in the race, with Holland leading and Mauri Rose running second, Rose set out to overtake his teammate. Rose proceeded to ignore car owner Lou Moore's 'EZ' signs from the pits and continued to push in pursuit of Holland. Finally Rose's car broke and Holland cruised home to victory. After the race Moore fired Rose on the spot for disobeying team orders.

---

# BOSTON MARATHON
# GÖSTA LEANDERSSON

The Boston Marathon is the oldest annual marathon in the world and dates back to 1897.

**Race Result:**

| | | |
|---|---|---|
| **1.** | **Gösta Leandersson (SWE)** | **2:31:50** |
| 2. | Victor Dyrgall (USA) | 2:34:42 |
| 3. | Louis White (USA) | 2:36:48 |

# BASKETBALL - BAA FINALS

4 - 2

Minneapolis Lakers                    Washington Capitols

## LEAGUE SUMMARY

The 1948-49 BAA season was the third and final season of the Basketball Association of America. In 1949 the BAA and National Basketball League merged to create the National Basketball Association or NBA. Today the NBA recognizes the three BAA seasons as part of its own history.

**Eastern Division:**

|   | Team | GP | W | L | PCT | GB |
|---|------|----|----|----|-----|-----|
| 1 | **Washington Capitols** | **60** | **38** | **22** | **.633** | - |
| 2 | New York Knicks | 60 | 32 | 28 | .533 | 6 |
| 3 | Baltimore Bullets | 60 | 29 | 31 | .483 | 9 |
| 4 | Philadelphia Warriors | 60 | 28 | 32 | .467 | 10 |
| 5 | Boston Celtics | 60 | 25 | 35 | .417 | 13 |
| 6 | Providence Steamrollers | 60 | 12 | 48 | .200 | 26 |

**Western Division:**

|   | Team | GP | W | L | PCT | GB |
|---|------|----|----|----|-----|-----|
| 1 | **Rochester Royals** | **60** | **45** | **15** | **.750** | - |
| 2 | Minneapolis Lakers | 60 | 44 | 16 | .733 | 1 |
| 3 | Chicago Stags | 60 | 38 | 22 | .633 | 7 |
| 4 | St. Louis Bombers | 60 | 29 | 31 | .483 | 16 |
| 5 | Fort Wayne Pistons | 60 | 22 | 38 | .367 | 23 |
| 6 | Indianapolis Jets | 60 | 18 | 42 | .300 | 27 |

**Statistics Leaders:**

|  | Player | Team | Stats |
|--|--------|------|-------|
| Points | George Mikan | Minneapolis Lakers | 1,698 |
| Assists | Bob Davies | Rochester Royals | 321 |
| FG% | Arnie Risen | Rochester Royals | .423 |
| FT% | Bob Feerick | Washington Capitols | .859 |

Note: Prior to the 1969-70 season league leaders in points and assists were determined by totals rather than averages.

# TENNIS - U.S. NATIONAL CHAMPIONSHIPS

**Mens Singles Champion - Pancho Gonzales - United States**
**Ladies Singles Champion - Margaret Osborne duPont - United States**

The 1949 U.S. National Championships (now known as the U.S. Open) took place on the outdoor grass courts at the West Side Tennis Club, Forest Hills in New York. The tournament ran from August 26 until September 5 and was the 69th staging of the U.S. National Championships.

### Men's Singles Final:

| Country | Player | Set 1 | Set 2 | Set 3 | Set 4 | Set 5 |
|---|---|---|---|---|---|---|
| United States | Pancho Gonzales | 16 | 2 | 6 | 6 | 6 |
| United States | Ted Schroeder | 18 | 6 | 1 | 2 | 4 |

### Women's Singles Final:

| Country | Player | Set 1 | Set 2 |
|---|---|---|---|
| United States | Margaret Osborne duPont | 6 | 6 |
| United States | Doris Hart | 4 | 1 |

### Men's Doubles Final:

| Country | Players | Set 1 | Set 2 | Set 3 |
|---|---|---|---|---|
| Australia | John Bromwich / Bill Sidwell | 6 | 6 | 6 |
| Australia | Frank Sedgman / George Worthington | 4 | 0 | 1 |

### Women's Doubles Final:

| Country | Players | Set 1 | Set 2 |
|---|---|---|---|
| United States | Louise Brough / Margaret Osborne duPont | 6 | 10 |
| United States | Shirley Fry / Doris Hart | 4 | 8 |

### Mixed Doubles Final:

| Country | Players | Set 1 | Set 2 | Set 3 |
|---|---|---|---|---|
| United States / South Africa | Louise Brough / Eric Sturgess | 4 | 6 | 7 |
| United States | Margaret Osborne duPont / Bill Talbert | 6 | 3 | 5 |

# THE COST OF LIVING

## "Blatz is Milwaukee's Finest Beer!"

"I've traveled all over the world," says Mr. McLaglen, Academy Award winner. "And nowhere else do they brew beer of Milwaukee quality. And, of all Milwaukee beers, none equals Blatz. It's Milwaukee's finest. I've lived there . . . and I ought to know."

**Blatz** BETTER TASTING BEER FOR THE 98th YEAR

BLATZ IS MILWAUKEE'S *first* BOTTLED BEER

## COMPARISON CHART

| | 1949 | 1949 Price Today (Including Inflation) | 2018 | Real Term % Change |
|---|---|---|---|---|
| Annual Income | $1,750 | $18,350 | $57,817 | +215.1% |
| House | $15,300 | $160,428 | $295,000 | +83.9% |
| Car | $2,150 | $22,544 | $33,560 | +48.9% |
| Gallon Of Gasoline | 25¢ | $2.62 | $2.43 | -7.2% |
| Gallon Of Milk | 30¢ | $3.15 | $4.42 | +40.3% |
| DC Comic Book | 10¢ | $1.05 | $3.99 | +280.0% |

# GROCERIES

| | |
|---|---:|
| Cloverbloom Butter (per lb) | 79¢ |
| Admiration Margarine (1lb) | 29¢ |
| Carnation Milk (3 large cans) | 39¢ |
| Mixed Sized Eggs (dozen) | 52¢ |
| Sunshine Hi-Ho Crackers (1lb box) | 29¢ |
| Gold Medal Flour (10lb bag) | 83¢ |
| Aged Red Wine Cheese (per lb) | 59¢ |
| Wisconsin Cheese (per lb) | 45¢ |
| Kellogg's Corn Flakes (12oz pkg.) | 18¢ |
| Quaker Oats (3lb box) | 35¢ |
| Empress Pure Strawberry Preserve (21oz jar) | 43¢ |
| Texas Oranges (5lb bag) | 39¢ |
| Winesap Apples (per lb) | 10¢ |
| Texas Grapefruit (x2) | 13¢ |
| Carton Tomatoes | 19¢ |
| Large 48 Size Lettuce (each) | 15¢ |
| Potatoes Economy Pack (10lb) | 49¢ |
| Red McClure Potatoes (5lb) | 23¢ |
| East Texas Cured Sw. Potatoes (per lb) | 6½¢ |
| Yellow Onions (3lb) | 10¢ |
| Carrots (2lb) | 15¢ |
| Del Monte Corn (303 can) | 19¢ |
| Lima Beans (can) | 25¢ |
| Green Giant Tender Peas (303 can) | 21¢ |
| Sirloin Steak (per lb) | 73¢ |
| Center Cuts Pork Chops (per lb) | 59¢ |
| Star Pure Pork Sausage (1lb) | 39¢ |
| Boneless Sliced Ham (per lb) | 99¢ |
| Swift's Premium Bacon (per lb) | 65¢ |
| Full Dressed Hen (per lb) | 49¢ |
| White Swan Salmon (tall can) | 75¢ |
| Skinner's Macaroni Or Spaghetti (7oz pkg.) | 10¢ |
| Comet Rice (12oz pkg.) | 15¢ |
| Heinz Baby Foods (3 cans) | 25¢ |
| Del Monte Ketchup (14oz bottle) | 19¢ |
| Hunt's Peaches (No.2½ can) | 29¢ |
| Maxwell House Coffee (1lb can) | 55¢ |
| Lipton's Tea (¼lb pkg.) | 57¢ |
| Full O' Gold Orange Juice (46oz can) | 33¢ |
| Texsun Grapefruit Juice (46oz can) | 19¢ |
| Palmolive Soap (2 bars) | 17¢ |
| Colgate Dental Cream | 75¢ |
| Tide - Duz Washing Powder (large box) | 27¢ |
| Crystal White Laundry Soap (2 giant bars) | 15¢ |
| Charmin Facial Tissues (2x 200 pkg.) | 25¢ |
| Scott Tissue (roll) | 10¢ |
| Bayer Aspirin (100) | 39¢ |
| Armour's Dash Dog Food (2x 1lb cans) | 25¢ |

# NOW IT'S
# ANTSY PANTIES FOR HER!
# ANTSY PANTS FOR HIM..

**HIS:** Boxer type shorts of luxurious all spun, washable rayon. Elastic waistband. Roomy saddle seat. White with red ants. Sizes: 28 to 46 inch waist. **$2⁵⁰**

**HERS:** Dainty Hollywood briefs of soft spun rayon jersey. Long-lasting elastic waist and legs. Washable. Colors: White pastel blue, tearose, or maize. Sizes: 3 to 8. **$1⁵⁰**

It's the biggest undercover news of the year—those big red ants are getting into everything these days! Practical and comfortable, too, in case you're wondering. Get yours at leading stores everywhere—or order direct today!

64

# CLOTHES

### Women's Clothing

| | |
|---|---|
| J. M. Dyer Navy Gabardine Spring Coat | $69.50 |
| Felt Beanie Hat | $1 |
| Sears 100% Wool Worsted Suit | $18 |
| Penney's Tailored Rayon Dress | $8.90 |
| Franklin's Blouse | $1.99 |
| Frances Shop Skirt | $3.75 |
| Yolande Slip | $4.95 |
| Sears Nylon Brassiere | $1.79 |
| Gossard Pantie Girdle | $3 |
| Gotham Gold Stripe Nylons | $1.95 |
| Lux-eez Nylon Panties | $2.50 |
| Marks Bros. Pigskin Gloves | $3.95 |
| Vitality Patent Shoes | $10.95 |
| Sears Moccasin Slippers | $1.98 |

### Men's Clothing

| | |
|---|---|
| McGregor Convertible Jacket | $27.50 |
| J. M. Dyer Overcoat | $16.75 |
| P. Samuels Stetson Stratoliner Hat | $10 |
| Harris & Jacobs Suit | $35.95 |
| Sears Pilgrim Sweater | $2.98 |
| Textron Sport Shirt | $7.95 |
| Manhattan White Broadcloth Shirt | $3.95 |
| Sears Broadcloth Boxer Shorts | 98¢ |
| Hill & Shipe Wing Tipped Shoes | $10.95 |
| Austin Smart Casual Shoes | $6.95 |
| Phoenix Nylon Socks (pair) | $1 |

# J.M.Dyer Co.

## **Paris** touches
## our Spring Coats

We've taken the most wearable of the French ideas, Americanized them and had them tailored into the most winning coats of any season.

**Left to right:**
The Directoire coat, after Mendel of Paris. In grey or black worsted sheen, 89.50.

Another Mendel silhouette, with full back focused at shoulder yoke. Navy, 65.00

From a Martial et Armand original. Grey or navy gabardine worn belted or flared, 69.50.

# TOYS

| | |
|---|---|
| Large DeLuxe Steel Wagon | $10.95 |
| Take Dolly Strolling Walker | $2.45 |
| 11 Inch Table Top Play Stove | $1.89 |
| Chime Wheels Stick Horse | $1.29 |
| Speedy Siren Fire Truck | $1.79 |
| Buffalo Bill Holster Set | 88¢ |
| Dolls House 8-pc Bedroom Set | 98¢ |
| 30 Inch Panda Bear | $5.95 |
| 11 Inch Rubber Doll | $1.89 |
| Official Size Scholastic Football | $2.62 |

# 7.2 Cubic Foot COLDSPOTS

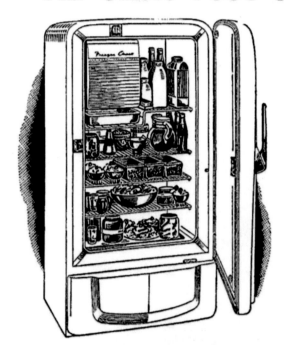

## Look At This Low Price!

# 179⁹⁵

**$5.00 Down - - $9:00 Month**
Usual Carrying Charge

- 5-Year Protection Plan
- 65 Ice Cubes, 6 lbs. 9 ozs.
- Holds 23 lbs. Frozen Food

Big 7.2 cubic foot Coldspots give you average family storage space . . . at a great dollar-savings! All steel cabinet of seamless construction. 5-year Protection Plan means extra guarantee for you . . . . backed by Sears. Stainless steel freezers store 22.3-pounds of food. A full 13.6-square feet of rust-resistant shelving. Plenty of sparkling ice cubes—65 cubes or 6-pounds, 9-ounces of ice. Look at the low, low price. Shop at Sears and Save!

# ELECTRICAL GOODS

| | |
|---|---|
| Emerson Big Screen 4-Way Television (11.2 inch) | $269.50 |
| Philco 7.2 Cu.Ft. Refrigerator | $199.50 |
| Coldspot 6 Cu.Ft. Freezer | $224.50 |
| Kenmore Washer ¼ H.P. Motor | $88.95 |
| Philco Single Room Air Conditioner | $349.50 |
| Dormeyer Food Mixer | $29.95 |
| Kenmore Vacuum Cleaner | $49.95 |
| Kenmore Electric Sewing Machine | $145 |
| Craftsman Lightweight Drill | $13.50 |
| 6-Way Floor Lamp | $7.88 |
| Wire-Recorder Radio In Mahogany Veneer Cabinet | $139.95 |
| Sears Table Model Radio | $9.95 |

MOTHER ADORES *dining out!*

# Special Sunday Dinner

Tomato Juice - - Pineapple and Cheese Salad

## CHOICE OF MEATS:

Baked Young Turkey with Oyster Dressing, Giblet Gravy and Cranberry Sauce, $1.25
Charcoal Broiled Half Spring Chicken .........................$1.50
Broiled or Fried Flounder, with Lemon and Butter Sauce ..............$1.25
Juicy Charcoal Broiled T-Bone Steak ........................$1.25
Broiled or Fried Trout with Tarter Sauce .......................$1.25
Juicy Charcoal Broiled Filet Mignon Steak .....................$1.25
Fried Spring Chicken on Cream Gravy .......................$1.00
Juicy Charcoal Broiled Club Steak .........................$1.00
Pan Fried Virginia Ham Steak with Natural Gravy ...............$1.00
Grilled Pork Chop with Onion Rings ........................$1.00

CHOICE OF POTATOES — Agratin Potatoes or Candied Yams

## Choice of (2) Heinz Vegetables:

| | | |
|---|---|---|
| Cut Wax Beans | Buttered Cauliflower | Creamed Asparagus |
| Spanish Corn | HOT CLOVERLEAF ROLLS | Early June Peas |

DESSERT: Heinz Pears in Heavy Syrup          DRINKS: Coffee, Tea or Milk

## —— ALA CARTE ——

Juicy Charcoal Broiled 16-oz. Sirloin Steak, Salad and French Fries .........$1.75
Juicy Charcoal Broiled 14-oz. T-Bone Steak, Salad and French Fries ........$1.50
Juicy Charcoal Broiled 9-oz. Filet Mignon Steak, Salad and French Fries .......$1.50
Juicy Charcoal Broiled 10-oz. Club Steak, Salad and French Fries ..........$1.25
Juicy Charcoal Broiled Mexican Inn Special Chopped Steak—
Salad and French Fries ...............................85c

—— All Our Meats Selected by Our City Meat Inspector - - Mr. Arthur Levi ——

## —— SEA FOODS ——

Broiled Flounder with Butter and Lemon Sauce, French Fries and Salad—$1.25-$1.50
Broiled or Fried Trout with Tarter Sauce, Salad and French Fries ..........$1.25
Extra Select Oysters with Salad and French Fries.......½ doz. 60c; 1 doz. $1.00
Jumbo Butterfly Fried Shrimp, Salad and French Fries ................75c
Fried Catfish, Salad and French Fries .........................75c
Jumbo Shrimp Cocktail .........75c     Oyster Cocktail ................75c

## —— SALADS ——

| | | | |
|---|---|---|---|
| Shrimp Salad ...............75c | Guacamole Salad .............60c |
| Chicken Salad ...............65c | Combination Salad ...........60c |
| Pineapple and Cheese .........75c | Fruit Salad ..................75c |

MEXICAN INN SPECIAL SALAD ................75c
ALL SALADS WITH BROCKLES DRESSING

### Mexican Food Is Our Specialty!

# MEXICAN INN

# OTHER ITEMS

| | |
|---|---|
| Kaiser Deluxe Car | $2509 |
| Packard Eight Club Sedan 130-HP | $2274 |
| Chevrolet Rebuilt Engine '37-'48 | $134 |
| Allstate High Speed Tires | $13.45 |
| Allstate 51-Plate Car Batteries | $14.95 |
| Wizard Super Twin Outboard Motor | $169.50 |
| Cinema Ticket | 55¢ |
| Sears Smart 5-pc. Porcelain Top Dinette Set | $69.95 |
| Simon Daniels Felt Base Rug (9x12) | $10 |
| Rural Mail Box | $1.98 |
| 16 Inch Lawn Mower | $15.95 |
| Sears Gas Range With New Roast-R-Oven | $139.50 |
| Sam Daiches 42-Piece Cutlery Service | $39.75 |
| Sears Day-Old Baby Chicks | 5¢ |
| Ancient Age 5-Year Old Straight Bourbon ($\frac{4}{5}$qt.) | $4.57 |
| Dixie Belle Gin (2x $\frac{4}{5}$qt.) | $5 |
| Ron Rico Bacardi Rum ($\frac{4}{5}$qt.) | $2.99 |
| Leading Brands Cigarettes (carton) | $1.73 |

Car shown—COMMANDER STARLIGHT COUPE

*Announcing*
## the new 1949 Studebakers
*A new vogue in interiors by Studebaker stylists!*

69

# U.S. COINS

| Official Circulated U.S. Coins | | Years Produced |
|---|---|---|
| Half-Cent | ½¢ | 1792 - 1857 |
| Cent (Penny) | 1¢ | 1793 - Present |
| 2-Cent | 2¢ | 1864 - 1873 |
| 3-Cent | 3¢ | 1851 - 1889 |
| Half-Dime | 5¢ | 1792 - 1873 |
| Five Cent Nickel | 5¢ | 1866 - Present |
| Dime | 10¢ | 1792 - Present |
| 20-Cent | 20¢ | 1875 - 1878 |
| Quarter | 25¢ | 1796 - Present |
| Half Dollar | 50¢ | 1794 - Present |
| Dollar Coin | $1 | 1794 - Present |
| Quarter Eagle | $2.50 | 1792 - 1929 |
| Three-Dollar Piece | $3 | 1854 - 1889 |
| Four-Dollar Piece | $4 | 1879 - 1880 |
| Half Eagle | $5 | 1795 – 1929 |
| Commemorative Half Eagle | $5 | 1980 - Present |
| Silver Eagle | $1 | 1986 - Present |
| Gold Eagle | $5 | 1986 - Present |
| Platinum Eagle | $10 - $100 | 1997 - Present |
| Double Eagle (Gold) | $20 | 1849 - 1933 |
| Half Union | $50 | 1915 |

# Comic Strips

THIMBLE THEATRE—Starring POPEYE

BARNEY GOOGLE AND SNUFFY SMITH

BLONDIE

HOMER HOOPEE